Tiny Tots

Edited By Donna Samworth

First published in Great Britian in 2016 by:

Coltsfoot Drive
Peterborough
PE2 9BF
Telephone: 01733 890066
Website: www.youngwriters.co.uk

All Rights Reserved
Book Design by Tim Christian
© Copyright Contributors 2016
SB ISBN 978-1-78624-260-0
Printed and bound in the UK by BookPrintingUK
Website: www.bookprintinguk.com
YB0270C

Young Writers was established in 1991 with the aim of encouraging writing skills in young people and giving them the opportunity to see their work in print. Poetry is a wonderful way to introduce young children to the idea of rhyme and rhythm and helps learning and development of communication, language and literacy skills.

'My First Poem' was created to introduce nursery and preschool children to this wonderful world of poetry. They were given a template to fill in with their own words, creating a poem that was all about them.

We are proud to present the resulting collection of personal and touching poems in this anthology, which can be treasured for years to come.

Jenni Bannister
Editorial Manager

Contents

All Saints Preschool, London

Ambar Monica Hierro Redonda Mclean (4)	1
Saad Khan (4)	2
Sanjpreet Kaur (4)	3
Jannat Noor Iqbal (3)	4
Joshua Nathaneal Earl-Singh (3)	5
Alessia Nicole Tudorache (4)	6
Hamza Khaliq (3)	7

Busy Bees Preschool, Brighton

Christopher Wood (4)	8
Liyana Malique (4)	9
Maxx Honhold (4)	10
Charlie Tarrant (4)	11
Lois Reed (3)	12
Isabella James (4)	13
Liam Court (4)	14
Alfie McCallum (3)	15
Maisie Jayne Wood (3)	16
Daisy Packer (4)	17
Blake Kew (3)	18
Nory Lovett (3)	19

Felixstowe Nursery School, Felixstowe

Tamia Baines-Roper (3)	20
Sapphire Andrews (2)	21
Noah Wardley (2)	22
Logan Ver-Haest (3)	23

Riley Ward (3)	24
Marlee Wakefield (4)	25
Fay Leslie (3)	26
Danny Wilson (2)	27
Freddie Cowan (3)	28
Poppy Garry (3)	29
Lily Dalton (3)	30
Lola Hughes (3)	31
Koryn Toby Moyes (3)	32
Miles Arthur Barclay (3)	33
Mia Darvill (2)	34
James Davies (3)	35
Amelia Barnes (3)	36
Eliza Paige Evans (3)	37

Harrietsham Preschool, Maidstone

Eve Holland (3)	38
Grace Thorneycroft (4)	39
Emilia Mitchell (4)	40
Buddy Eeles (3)	41
Oscar Wesson Arthur Martin (4)	42
Erin Vinnicombe (4)	43

Jumping Jellybeans Preschool, Poole

Alfie Davis (4)	44
Elexia Louise Fitzgerald (3)	45

Leicester Montessori School, Leicester

Noel Cassidy (4)	46
Rhylie Shornyk (3)	47
Hafsa Shabudin (3)	48
Khadeejah Dhariwal (4)	49
Darsh Patel (3)	50
Elijah Webbe (3)	51

Little Angels, Peterborough

Fayth Pragliola (4)	52
Layla Gee (4)	53
Dylan Thomas Nicholson (3)	54
Emma Turner (4)	55

Little Angels, Sittingbourne

Vienna Bird (4)	56
George Robbins (3)	57
Sophia Bicker (4)	58
Finley Brunger (4)	59
Logan Hook (4)	60
Kourtney Pout (4)	61
Emily Corbin (3)	62

Little Oaks Nursery, Boston

Riley Smith (4)	63
Maisie Pope (4)	64
Paige Davidson (3)	65
Shayla Woods (4)	66
Alex Newson (3)	67
Ruby Davidson (3)	68
Miley Chloe Jasmine Hancock (3)	69
Lenny Teft (4)	70
Taylor Adams (3)	71
Maddison Messenger (3)	72
Reggi Vernon (4)	73
Lillie Rowett (4)	74

Amelia Grace Keal (3)	75
Andrew Leyland (3)	76
Emilija Rimkute (3)	77
Chloe Dent (4)	78
Jacob Moore (3)	79
Alex Done (4)	80

Loughgall Playgroup, Armagh

Ella George (4)	81
Johnny Patterson (4)	82
Farrah Forbes (3)	83
Sophia Calvin (3)	84
Jodie E White (4)	85

Nassington Preschool, Peterborough

Arthur Homan (4)	86
Noah Dorward (4)	87
Daisy Dorward (4)	88
Lucy Jenkinson (4)	89
Lucy Earl (3)	90
Matilda Rickwood (3)	91

Orton St Johns Preschool, Peterborough

Alfie Thomas (3)	92
Dennis Jack Herbert (4)	93
Alison Bradbury (3)	94
Jamie-Leigh Cooper (2)	95
Charlie Mark Uff (3)	96
Crystal Bailey (3)	97
Joshua Allcorn (3)	98
Morgan Robert Glynn (3)	99
Dawid Olszowski (3)	100
Harry Jacob Gray (3)	101

Maddison Louise Sinnott Brooker (3)	102
Shara Brewer (3)	103

Oulton Abbey Playgroup, Stone

George Carnes (2)	104
Thomas Gadsbey (3)	105
Tilly Follwell (2)	106
Monty Hartwell Priest (3)	107
Stanley Roycroft (4)	108
Annabel Rose Dickson (3)	109
Reuben Seth Hartley Dawson (4)	110
Charlotte-Lucy Ogle (3)	111
Lillie Rose Ames (3)	112
Arthur Seabridge (3)	113
Connie Seabridge (2)	114
Joshua Follwell (4)	115

Penguin Preschool, Great Yarmouth

Alexie Cook (3)	116
Melissa Griffin (4)	117
Liara McKay (4)	118
Lola-Rose Ria Savage (3)	119
Braydon Dean Price (4)	120
Jordan Whawell (3)	121
Kelvin Williams (3)	122
Madison Lily Skevington (4)	123
Gemma Rose Townsend (3)	124
Olly Beggs (3)	125

Roborough Preschool, Plymouth

Joshua Goldsmith (4)	126
Jacob Bishop (3)	127

Runcton Holme Preschool, King's Lynn

George Wright (4)	128
Jack Brighton (3)	129
William Wedd-Johnson (3)	130
James William David Garnham (2)	131
Phyllis Caley Garnham (3)	132

Salendine Nook Preschool, Huddersfield

Riley Weekes (4)	133
Olivia Margrave (2)	134
Elijah Hall (4)	135
Ava McCafferty (3)	136
Rimshah Shafi (4)	137
Jorja Leah Lister (4)	138
Jonah Quinn (4)	139
Joey Thwaites (4)	140
Kaleb Wykes (4)	141
Kianne Wykes (2)	142
Nathan Blakemore (4)	143
Olivia Rose Mellor (3)	144
Leo James Smith (3)	145
Aayan Khaliq Uddin (3)	146
Alfie Leach (2)	147
Billy Broster (2)	148

Shining Stars Preschool Nursery, Peterborough

Asma Ahmed (4)	149
Sara Yasin (3)	150
Amelia Ul-Haq (4)	151
Asad Rashid (4)	152

South Brent Preschool, South Brent

Lacey-Jaie Burridge (4)	153

Amelia Herriott (3)	154
Lilah Schaefer (3)	155
Ella Rose Lane (2)	156
Evelyn Scott (3)	157
Jack Jellicoe (3)	158
Lacey Davies (4)	159
Kaitlyn Hayter (3)	160

Steeple Claydon Nursery, Buckingham

Reece Cook (4)	161
Aston Field (2)	162
Kai Piosek-Smith (2)	163
Evan Timothy Wedley (4)	164
Brennan Michael Donald Lee (3)	165
Jamie Mills-Baughan (2)	166
Kaylee Ann Paxton (4)	167
Annabelle Gould (2)	168
Harry Carroll (3)	169
Oliver Matthias (4)	170
Jacob Butler (3)	171
Rosie Joy Fenables (3)	172

The Links Nursery, Stockton-On-Tees

Bailey Coterill (3)	173
Phebe Crockett (4)	174
Sorcha Bond (4)	175
Oliver Daly (4)	176
Joseph Horlock (3)	177
Ted Cartman (3)	178
Alexander Owen Pindor (3)	179
Jamie Carter (3)	180
Finnan Brian Hanrahan (4)	181
Evie Jessica Peters (3)	182
Ava Corner (4)	183
Emelia Wray (3)	184

The Willows, Didcot

Max William Alan Foster (3)	185
Indiana Jay Bennett (3)	186
Kalina Kantyka (3)	187
Ffion Blundell (3)	188
Lauren Grace (3)	189
Harry Austin (3)	190
Ava Butler (3)	191
Pippa McGibbon (3)	192
Jasmiina Alhaddad (3)	193
Jack Bolton (3)	194
Isabella Burchell (3)	195
Milä Antonia Jennifer Woods (3)	196
Charlie Owen (3)	197
Cara Duffy (3)	198

Tiny Tots Corner Playgroup, Armagh

Annabel Thompson (3)	199
Myah Sarah Morrison (4)	200
Isaac Gardiner (4)	201
Pippa Watson (3)	202
Jenny Agnew (4)	203
Chloe Deering (4)	204
Dylan Robinson (4)	205
Samuel Gillespie (4)	206

Voyage @ Flash Ley, Stafford

Jaida Allam (3)	207
Conor Richard Norman Robinson (3)	208
Abbie Grace Judith Davis (3)	209
Maisy Michelle McCracken (3)	210
Saffron Sheila Brenda Lowe (4)	211
Grace Ghaley (3)	212
Niamh Capewell (3)	213

The Poems

My First Poem

My name is **Ambar** and I go to preschool,
My best friend is **Sanjpreet**, who is really cool.
I watch **Disney** on TV,
Playing **dressing up** is lots of fun for me.
I just love **strawberries** to eat,
And sometimes **raspberries** for a treat.
Blue is a colour I like a lot,
My **Elsa stickers** are the best present I ever got.
My favourite person is **Mum**, who is a gem,
So this, my first poem, is just for them!

Ambar Monica Hierro Redonda Mclean (4)

All Saints Preschool, London

My First Poem

My name is **Saad** and I go to preschool,
My best friend is **Ambar**, who is really cool.
I watch **Megaforce** on TV,
Playing **with trains** is lots of fun for me.
I just love **salad** to eat,
And sometimes **crisps** for a treat.
Green and blue are colours I like a lot,
My **crayons and hat** are the best presents I ever got.
My favourite person is **my sister**, who is a gem,
So this, my first poem, is just for them!

Saad Khan (4)
All Saints Preschool, London

My First Poem

My name is **Sanjpreet** and I go to preschool,
My best friend is **Ambar**, who is really cool.
I watch **101 Dalmations** on TV,
Playing **dressing up like Elsa** is lots of fun for me.
I just love **chocolate bread** to eat,
And sometimes **a chicken burger** for a treat.
Blue is a colour I like a lot,
My **Elsa doll** is the best present I ever got.
My favourite person is **my sister**, who is a gem,
So this, my first poem, is just for them!

Sanjpreet Kaur (4)
All Saints Preschool, London

My First Poem

My name is **Jannat** and I go to preschool,
My best friend is **Casey**, who is really cool.
I watch **Peppa Pig** on TV,
Playing **on bikes** is lots of fun for me.
I just love **chicken** to eat,
And sometimes **a Kinder egg** for a treat.
Red is a colour I like a lot,
My **Frozen perfume** is the best present I ever got.
My favourite people are **Mummy and Daddy**, who are gems,
So this, my first poem, is just for them!

Jannat Noor Iqbal (3)

All Saints Preschool, London

My First Poem

My name is Joshua and I go to preschool,
My best friend is Linda, who is really cool.
I watch CBeebies on TV,
Playing with cars is lots of fun for me.
I just love salad to eat,
And sometimes ice cream for a treat.
Yellow is a colour I like a lot,
My horse is the best present I ever got.
My favourite person is Mummy, who is a gem,
So this, my first poem, is just for them!

Joshua Nathaneal Earl-Singh (3)

All Saints Preschool, London

My First Poem

My name is **Alessia** and I go to preschool,
My best friend is **Sofiya**, who is really cool.
I watch **ponies** on TV,
Playing **with teddies** is lots of fun for me.
I just love **spaghetti** to eat,
And sometimes **apples** for a treat.
Pink is a colour I like a lot,
My **crown** is the best present I ever got.
My favourite person is **my sister**, who is a gem,
So this, my first poem, is just for them!

Alessia Nicole Tudorache (4)

All Saints Preschool, London

My First Poem

My name is **Hamza** and I go to preschool,
My best friends are **Damian and Jayden**, who are really cool.
I watch **Baymax** on TV,
Playing **robots** is lots of fun for me.
I just love **banana** to eat,
And sometimes **burgers** for a treat.
Green is a colour I like a lot,
My **big Baymax** is the best present I ever got.
My favourite person is **Grandad**, who is a gem,
So this, my first poem, is just for them!

Hamza Khaliq (3)

All Saints Preschool, London

My First Poem

My name is **Christopher** and I go to preschool,
My best friend is **Safwan**, who is really cool.
I watch **Transformers** on TV,
Playing **with Play-Doh** is lots of fun for me.
I just love **sausage rolls** to eat,
And sometimes **sausage rolls again** for a treat.
Blue is a colour I like a lot,
My **PAW Patrol** is the best present I ever got.
My favourite person is **Safwan**, who is a gem,
So this, my first poem, is just for them!

Christopher Wood (4)

Busy Bees Preschool, Brighton

My First Poem

My name is **Liyana** and I go to preschool,
My best friend is **Maxx**, who is really cool.
I watch **Teletubbies** on TV,
Playing **with Peppa Pig** is lots of fun for me.
I just love **crisps** to eat,
And sometimes **squishy gummy bears** for a treat.
Red is a colour I like a lot,
My **police toy** is the best present I ever got.
My favourite person is **my daddy**, who is a gem,
So this, my first poem, is just for them!

Liyana Malique (4)
Busy Bees Preschool, Brighton

My First Poem

My name is **Maxx** and I go to preschool,
My best friend is **Liyana**, who is really cool.
I watch **Teletubbies** on TV,
Playing **with Robo Dog** is lots of fun for me.
I just love **crispies** to eat,
And sometimes **sweeties** for a treat.
Red is a colour I like a lot,
My **Thunderbird number five** is the best present I ever got.
My favourite person is **Liyana**, who is a gem,
So this, my first poem, is just for them!

Maxx Honhold (4)
Busy Bees Preschool, Brighton

My First Poem

My name is Charlie and I go to preschool,
My best friend is Amelie, who is really cool.
I watch dinosaur films on TV,
Playing dinosaurs is lots of fun for me.
I just love Shreddies to eat,
And sometimes sweeties for a treat.
Green and blue are colours I like a lot,
My big, big shark is the best present I ever got.
My favourite person is my big brother,
who is a gem,
So this, my first poem, is just for them!

Charlie Tarrant (4)

Busy Bees Preschool, Brighton

My First Poem

My name is **Lois** and I go to preschool,
My best friend is **Amelie**, who is really cool.
I watch **Peppa Pig** on TV,
Playing **with dollies** is lots of fun for me.
I just love **Cheestrings** to eat,
And sometimes **sweets** for a treat.
Pink is a colour I like a lot,
My **dolly** is the best present I ever got.
My favourite person is **Mrs Rayner**, who is a gem,
So this, my first poem, is just for them!

Lois Reed (3)
Busy Bees Preschool, Brighton

My First Poem

My name is **Bella** and I go to preschool,
My best friend is **Evelynn**, who is really cool.
I watch **My Little Pony** on TV,
Playing **with cars** is lots of fun for me.
I just love **strawberries** to eat,
And sometimes **sweets** for a treat.
Purple is a colour I like a lot,
My **My Little Pony** is the best present I ever got.
My favourite person is **Mummy**, who is a gem,
So this, my first poem, is just for them!

Isabella James (4)

Busy Bees Preschool, Brighton

My First Poem

My name is **Liam** and I go to preschool,
My best friend is **Alfie**, who is really cool.
I watch **Thomas and friends** on TV,
Playing **with toy trains** is lots of fun for me.
I just love **pizza** to eat,
And sometimes **chocolate cake** for a treat.
Black is a colour I like a lot,
My **Thomas Take 'n' Play set** is the best present I ever got.
My favourite people are **Mummy and Daddy**, who are gems,
So this, my first poem, is just for them!

Liam Court (4)
Busy Bees Preschool, Brighton

My First Poem

My name is Alfie and I go to preschool,
My best friend is Liam, who is really cool.
I watch The Lion Guard on TV,
Playing doctors is lots of fun for me.
I just love cake to eat,
And sometimes Kinder eggs for a treat.
Pink is a colour I like a lot,
My monster thing is the best present I ever got.
My favourite person is Liam, who is a gem,
So this, my first poem, is just for them!

Alfie McCallum (3)

Busy Bees Preschool, Brighton

My First Poem

My name is **Maisie** and I go to preschool,
My best friend is **Daisy**, who is really cool.
I watch **princesses** on TV,
Playing **choo-choo trains** is lots of fun for me.
I just love **McDonald's** to eat,
And sometimes **carrots** for a treat.
Pink is a colour I like a lot,
My **Doc McStuffins** is the best present I ever got.
My favourite person is **Daisy**, who is a gem,
So this, my first poem, is just for them!

Maisie Jayne Wood (3)
Busy Bees Preschool, Brighton

My First Poem

My name is **Daisy** and I go to preschool,
My best friend is **Maisie**, who is really cool.
I watch **Mother Goose Club** on TV,
Playing **babies** is lots of fun for me.
I just love **cucumber** to eat,
And sometimes **chocolate** for a treat.
Red is a colour I like a lot,
My **big baby that crawls** is the best present I ever got.
My favourite person is **Maisie**, who is a gem,
So this, my first poem, is just for them!

Daisy Packer (4)

Busy Bees Preschool, Brighton

My First Poem

My name is **Blake** and I go to preschool,
My best friend is **Mummy**, who is really cool.
I watch **Sonic** on TV,
Playing **with cars** is lots of fun for me.
I just love **toast** to eat,
And sometimes **sweets** for a treat.
Black is a colour I like a lot,
My **Pig Goes Pop** is the best present I ever got.
My favourite person is **Mummy**, who is a gem,
So this, my first poem, is just for them!

Blake Kew (3)
Busy Bees Preschool, Brighton

My First Poem

My name is Nory and I go to preschool,
My best friend is my lovely mum, who is really cool.
I watch PAW Patrol on TV,
Playing aeroplanes is lots of fun for me.
I just love carrots to eat,
And sometimes Kinder eggs for a treat.
Pink and purple are colours I like a lot,
My China, the dog, is the best present I ever got.
My favourite person is Mum again, who is a gem,
So this, my first poem, is just for them!

Nory Lovett (3)

Busy Bees Preschool, Brighton

My First Poem

My name is **Tamia** and I go to preschool,
My best friend is **Lexie**, who is really cool.
I watch **Peppa Pig** on TV,
Playing **with my Play-Doh** is lots of fun for me.
I just love **apples** to eat,
And sometimes **red sweets** for a treat.
Blue is a colour I like a lot,
My **Peppa Pig** is the best present I ever got.
My favourite people are **Nanny and Grandad**, who are gems,
So this, my first poem, is just for them!

Tamia Baines-Roper (3)
Felixstowe Nursery School, Felixstowe

My First Poem

My name is **Sapphire** and I go to preschool,
My best friend is **Miss Jones**, who is really cool.
I watch **penguins** on TV,
Playing **with my Noddy toys** is lots of
fun for me.
I just love **porridge and honey** to eat,
And sometimes **going to the beach** for a treat.
Pink is a colour I like a lot,
My **bumpy dog** is the best present I ever got.
My favourite person is **Mummy**, who is a gem,
So this, my first poem, is just for them!

Sapphire Andrews (2)
Felixstowe Nursery School, Felixstowe

My First Poem

My name is **Noah** and I go to preschool,
My best friend is **Annie**, who is really cool.
I watch **Spider-Man** on TV,
Playing **with Spider-Man toys** is lots of fun for me.
I just love **hot dogs and tomato sauce** to eat,
And sometimes **lollipops** for a treat.
Red is a colour I like a lot,
My **motorbike balance bike** is the best present I ever got.
My favourite person is **Mummy**, who is a gem,
So this, my first poem, is just for them!

Noah Wardley (2)
Felixstowe Nursery School, Felixstowe

My First Poem

My name is **Logan** and I go to preschool,
My best friend is **Riley**, who is really cool.
I watch **Peppa Pig and George** on TV,
Playing **with cars** is lots of fun for me.
I just love **biscuits** to eat,
And sometimes **black and white chocolate** for a treat.
Pink is a colour I like a lot,
My **transporter** is the best present I ever got.
My favourite person is **Mummy**, who is a gem,
So this, my first poem, is just for them!

Logan Ver-Haest (3)

Felixstowe Nursery School, Felixstowe

My First Poem

My name is **Riley** and I go to preschool,
My best friend is **Freddie**, who is really cool.
I watch **aliens and Minions** on TV,
Playing **with diggers and cars** is lots of fun for me.
I just love **crumpets** to eat,
And sometimes **pineapple** for a treat.
Red is a colour I like a lot,
My **dinosaurs** are the best present I ever got.
My favourite people are **Daddy, Mummy and Erica**, who are gems,
So this, my first poem, is just for them!

Riley Ward (3)
Felixstowe Nursery School, Felixstowe

My First Poem

My name is Marlee and I go to preschool,
My best friend is Lily, who is really cool.
I watch Minions on TV,
Playing with Play-Doh and with animals is lots of fun for me.
I just love bananas, oranges and apples to eat,
And sometimes Mummy takes me to the park with chocolate for a treat.
Red and orange are colours I like a lot,
My Woody is the best present I ever got.
My favourite people are Nanny and Tamsin, who are gems,
So this, my first poem, is just for them!

Marlee Wakefield (4)
Felixstowe Nursery School, Felixstowe

My First Poem

My name is Fay and I go to preschool,
My best friend is Ada, who is really cool.
I watch CBeebies on TV,
Playing with my My Little Pony ball is lots of fun for me.
I just love sweetcorn to eat,
And sometimes playing with Play-Doh for a treat.
Red is a colour I like a lot,
My shopping basket is the best present I ever got.
My favourite person is Mummy, who is a gem,
So this, my first poem, is just for them!

Fay Leslie (3)

Felixstowe Nursery School, Felixstowe

My First Poem

My name is **Danny** and I go to preschool,
My best friend is **Nanny**, who is really cool.
I watch **Peppa Pig** on TV,
Playing **with cars** is lots of fun for me.
I just love **dippy eggs** to eat,
And sometimes **crisps** for a treat.
Pink is a colour I like a lot,
My **bike** is the best present I ever got.
My favourite person is **Daddy**, who is a gem,
So this, my first poem, is just for them!

Danny Wilson (2)
Felixstowe Nursery School, Felixstowe

My First Poem

My name is **Freddie** and I go to preschool,
My best friend is **Riley**, who is really cool.
I watch **Peppa Pig** on TV,
Playing **on my green bike** is lots of fun for me.
I just love **chicken nuggets and chips** to eat,
And sometimes **chocolate cake with chocolate on the bottom** for a treat.
Red is a colour I like a lot,
My **drum** is the best present I ever got.
My favourite person is **my mummy**, who is a gem,
So this, my first poem, is just for them!

Freddie Cowan (3)

Felixstowe Nursery School, Felixstowe

My First Poem

My name is **Poppy** and I go to preschool,
My best friend is **Mrs Durrant**, who is really cool.
I watch **Peppa Pig** on TV,
Playing **with my Peppa Pigs** is lots of fun for me.
I just love **peanut butter sandwich** to eat,
And sometimes **banana sweets** for a treat.
Pink is a colour I like a lot,
My **toy kitchen** is the best present I ever got.
My favourite person is **my mummy**, who is a gem,
So this, my first poem, is just for them!

Poppy Garry (3)

Felixstowe Nursery School, Felixstowe

My First Poem

My name is Lily and I go to preschool,
My best friend is Marlee, who is really cool.
I watch Dora on TV,
Playing with my sister, Mia, is lots of fun for me.
I just love mashed potato and gravy to eat,
And sometimes chocolate for a treat.
Orange is a colour I like a lot,
My purple bike is the best present I ever got.
My favourite person is my mummy, who is a gem,
So this, my first poem, is just for them!

Lily Dalton (3)
Felixstowe Nursery School, Felixstowe

My First Poem

My name is Lola and I go to preschool,
My best friend is Freddie, who is really cool.
I watch Peppa Pig on TV,
Playing on my purple bike with my sister, Rachel, is lots of fun for me.
I just love chicken nuggets, chips and tomato sauce to eat,
And sometimes I go to the beach for a treat.
Pink is a colour I like a lot,
My purple bike is the best present I ever got.
My favourite person is Nanny, who is a gem,
So this, my first poem, is just for them!

Lola Hughes (3)
Felixstowe Nursery School, Felixstowe

My First Poem

My name is Koryn and I go to preschool,
My best friend is Poppa, who is really cool.
I watch PAW Patrol and Team Umizoomi on TV,
Playing with tractors is lots of fun for me.
I just love spaghetti and noodles to eat,
And sometimes lollipops for a treat.
Orange is a colour I like a lot,
My guitar is the best present I ever got.
My favourite person is Blake, who is a gem,
So this, my first poem, is just for them!

Koryn Toby Moyes (3)

Felixstowe Nursery School, Felixstowe

My First Poem

My name is **Miles** and I go to preschool,
My best friend is **Livia, my sister**, who is really cool.
I watch **PAW Patrol** on TV,
Playing **with my train track** is lots of fun for me.
I just love **biscuits dipped in tea** to eat,
And sometimes **worm sweets** for a treat.
Pink is a colour I like a lot,
My **train track** is the best present I ever got.
My favourite people are **Livia and Brandon**, who are gems,
So this, my first poem, is just for them!

Miles Arthur Barclay (3)

Felixstowe Nursery School, Felixstowe

My First Poem

My name is **Mia** and I go to preschool,
My best friend is **Lily**, who is really cool.
I watch **Dora** on TV,
Playing **babies** is lots of fun for me.
I just love **crispies and biscuits** to eat,
And sometimes **a pickle sandwich** for a treat.
Red, yellow, pink and green are colours I like a lot,
My **blue and white scooter** is the best present I ever got.
My favourite person is **Mummy**, who is a gem,
So this, my first poem, is just for them!

Mia Darvill (2)

Felixstowe Nursery School, Felixstowe

My First Poem

My name is **James** and I go to preschool,
My best friend is **Freddie**, who is really cool.
I watch **Peppa Pig and Team Umizoomi** on TV,
Playing **with my turtle** is lots of fun for me.
I just love **green apples** to eat,
And sometimes **lollies at the pier** for a treat.
Red is a colour I like a lot,
My **red bike** is the best present I ever got.
My favourite person is **Mummy**, who is a gem,
So this, my first poem, is just for them!

James Davies (3)
Felixstowe Nursery School, Felixstowe

My First Poem

My name is **Amelia** and I go to preschool,
My best friend is **my sister, Kayla**, who is really cool.
I watch **Peppa Pig** on TV,
Playing **with Barbies** is lots of fun for me.
I just love **spaghetti** to eat,
And sometimes **marshmallow** for a treat.
Pink is a colour I like a lot,
My **high chair for my baby** is the best present I ever got.
My favourite person is **Grandma**, who is a gem,
So this, my first poem, is just for them!

Amelia Barnes (3)
Felixstowe Nursery School, Felixstowe

My First Poem

My name is **Eliza** and I go to preschool,
My best friend is **my mummy**, who is really cool.
I watch **Alice in Wonderland** on TV,
Playing **with dollies and their clothes** is lots of fun for me.
I just love **potatoes, chocolate and strawberry ice cream** to eat,
And sometimes **cucumber** for a treat.
Pink is a colour I like a lot,
My **pink and yellow noisy bike** is the best present I ever got.
My favourite person is **my mummy**, who is a gem,
So this, my first poem, is just for them!

Eliza Paige Evans (3)
Felixstowe Nursery School, Felixstowe

My First Poem

My name is **Eve** and I go to preschool,
My best friend is **Grace**, who is really cool.
I watch **The Little Mermaid** on TV,
Playing **with my Tinkerbell doll** is lots of fun for me.
I just love **pasta** to eat,
And sometimes **sweets** for a treat.
Pink is a colour I like a lot,
My **Elsa doll** is the best present I ever got.
My favourite person is **Daddy**, who is a gem,
So this, my first poem, is just for them!

Eve Holland (3)
Harrietsham Preschool, Maidstone

My First Poem

My name is **Grace** and I go to preschool,
My best friend is **Eve**, who is really cool.
I watch **Peppa Pig** on TV,
Playing **babies** is lots of fun for me.
I just love **soup** to eat,
And sometimes **sweets** for a treat.
Pink is a colour I like a lot,
My **doll** is the best present I ever got.
My favourite person is **Mummy**, who is a gem,
So this, my first poem, is just for them!

Grace Thorneycroft (4)

Harrietsham Preschool, Maidstone

My First Poem

My name is Emilia and I go to preschool,
My best friend is Sally, who is really cool.
I watch Peppa Pig on TV,
Playing cupcakes is lots of fun for me.
I just love sweets to eat,
And sometimes a kiwi fruit for a treat.
Pink is a colour I like a lot,
My Bear Bear is the best present I ever got.
My favourite person is Mummy, who is a gem,
So this, my first poem, is just for them!

Emilia Mitchell (4)

Harrietsham Preschool, Maidstone

My First Poem

My name is Buddy and I go to preschool,
My best friends are Chloe and Olly,
who are really cool.
I watch PAW Patrol on TV,
Playing bad guys is lots of fun for me.
I just love apples to eat,
And sometimes chocolate for a treat.
Blue is a colour I like a lot,
My Iron Man is the best present I ever got.
My favourite person is Mummy, who is a gem,
So this, my first poem, is just for them!

Buddy Eeles (3)

Harrietsham Preschool, Maidstone

My First Poem

My name is **Oscar** and I go to preschool,
My best friends are **Jimmy and Maisy**, who are really cool.
I watch **Stickman and Cars** on TV,
Playing **with cars and puzzles** is lots of fun for me.
I just love **pasta with my favourite sauce** to eat,
And sometimes **blueberry pancakes** for a treat.
Red, blue, orange and white are colours I like a lot,
My **book 'The Highway Rat'** is the best present I ever got.
My favourite person is **Daddy**, who is a gem,
So this, my first poem, is just for them!

Oscar Wesson Arthur Martin (4)
Harrietsham Preschool, Maidstone

My First Poem

My name is **Erin** and I go to preschool,
My best friend is **Amy**, who is really cool.
I watch **Stampy, My Little Pony and Frozen** on TV,
Playing **Minecraft** is lots of fun for me.
I just love **pizza** to eat,
And sometimes **sweets** for a treat.
Pink is a colour I like a lot,
My **bike** is the best present I ever got.
My favourite person is **Mummy**, who is a gem,
So this, my first poem, is just for them!

Erin Vinnicombe (4)

Harrietsham Preschool, Maidstone

My First Poem

My name is **Alfie** and I go to preschool,
My best friends are **Ollie and Bentley**, who are really cool.
I watch **dinosaurs and Shaun the Sheep** on TV,
Playing **superheroes** is lots of fun for me.
I just love **Coco Pops and cake** to eat,
And sometimes **we go to Longleat** for a treat.
Blue is a colour I like a lot,
My **balance bike** is the best present I ever got.
My favourite person is **my mummy**, who is a gem,
So this, my first poem, is just for them!

Alfie Davis (4)
Jumping Jellybeans Preschool, Poole

My First Poem

My name is Elexia and I go to preschool,
My best friend is Aliona, who is really cool.
I watch My Little Pony on TV,
Playing with my Playmobil is lots of fun for me.
I just love pizza to eat,
And sometimes fruit for a treat.
Purple is a colour I like a lot,
My Playmobil is the best present I ever got.
My favourite person is Daddy, who is a gem,
So this, my first poem, is just for them!

Elexia Louise Fitzgerald (3)

Jumping Jellybeans Preschool, Poole

My First Poem

My name is **Noel** and I go to preschool,
My best friend is **Elijah**, who is really cool.
I watch **Batman** on TV,
Playing **with cars** is lots of fun for me.
I just love **sausages** to eat,
And sometimes **chocolate** for a treat.
Blue is a colour I like a lot,
My **Xbox** is the best present I ever got.
My favourite person is **my daddy**, who is a gem,
So this, my first poem, is just for them!

Noel Cassidy (4)
Leicester Montessori School, Leicester

My First Poem

My name is **Rhylie** and I go to preschool,
My best friend is **Layla**, who is really cool.
I watch **Topsy and Tim** on TV,
Playing **cleaning** is lots of fun for me.
I just love **chicken** to eat,
And sometimes **sweets** for a treat.
Black is a colour I like a lot,
My **car** is the best present I ever got.
My favourite person is **Noel**, who is a gem,
So this, my first poem, is just for them!

Rhylie Shornyk (3)
Leicester Montessori School, Leicester

My First Poem

My name is Hafsa and I go to preschool,
My best friend is Rafael, who is really cool.
I watch cartoons on TV,
Playing with blocks is lots of fun for me.
I just love pasta to eat,
And sometimes sweets for a treat.
Red is a colour I like a lot,
My puzzle is the best present I ever got.
My favourite person is Mum, who is a gem,
So this, my first poem, is just for them!

Hafsa Shabudin (3)

Leicester Montessori School, Leicester

My First Poem

My name is **Khadeejah** and I go to preschool,
My best friend is **Layla**, who is really cool.
I watch **Peppa Pig** on TV,
Playing **with Play-Doh** is lots of fun for me.
I just love **beans on toast** to eat,
And sometimes **cake** for a treat.
Red is a colour I like a lot,
My **Cinderella game** is the best present I ever got.
My favourite person is **Lauren**, who is a gem,
So this, my first poem, is just for them!

Khadeejah Dhariwal (4)

Leicester Montessori School, Leicester

My First Poem

My name is **Darsh** and I go to preschool,
My best friend is **Noel**, who is really cool.
I watch **Fireman Sam** on TV,
Playing **hairdressers** is lots of fun for me.
I just love **eggs** to eat,
And sometimes **chocolate** for a treat.
Red is a colour I like a lot,
My **car** is the best present I ever got.
My favourite person is **my mummy**, who is a gem,
So this, my first poem, is just for them!

Darsh Patel (3)

Leicester Montessori School, Leicester

My First Poem

My name is **Elijah** and I go to preschool,
My best friend is **Darsh**, who is really cool.
I watch **Nemo** on TV,
Playing **with Minions** is lots of fun for me.
I just love **beans** to eat,
And sometimes **sweets** for a treat.
Orange is a colour I like a lot,
My **Thomas and Friends** is the best present I ever got.
My favourite person is **my dad**, who is a gem,
So this, my first poem, is just for them!

Elijah Webbe (3)
Leicester Montessori School, Leicester

My First Poem

My name is **Fayth** and I go to preschool,
My best friend is **Dylan**, who is really cool.
I watch **Let It Go** on TV,
Playing **with Anna** is lots of fun for me.
I just love **potatoes** to eat,
And sometimes **sweets** for a treat.
Pink is a colour I like a lot,
My **Mickey Mouse dressing up** is the best present I ever got.
My favourite person is **Jenai**, who is a gem,
So this, my first poem, is just for them!

Fayth Pragliola (4)

Little Angels, Peterborough

My First Poem

My name is **Layla** and I go to preschool,
My best friend is **Dylan**, who is really cool.
I watch **CBeebies and The Simpsons** on TV,
Playing **with all my toys** is lots of fun for me.
I just love **chicken** to eat,
And sometimes **ice cream with strawberry sauce on it** for a treat.
Pink and blue are colours I like a lot,
My **piano** is the best present I ever got.
My favourite person is **Tia**, who is a gem,
So this, my first poem, is just for them!

Layla Gee (4)

Little Angels, Peterborough

My First Poem

My name is **Dylan** and I go to preschool,
My best friend is **Layla**, who is really cool.
I watch **Nick Jr.** on TV,
Playing **the hippotomus game** is lots of fun for me.
I just love **sausage and beans** to eat,
And sometimes **chocolate** for a treat.
Blue is a colour I like a lot,
My **piggy** is the best present I ever got.
My favourite person is **Mummy**, who is a gem,
So this, my first poem, is just for them!

Dylan Thomas Nicholson (3)

Little Angels, Peterborough

My First Poem

My name is **Emma** and I go to preschool,
My best friend is **Jenai**, who is really cool.
I watch **doggy** on TV,
Playing **with magnetic letters** is lots of fun for me.
I just love **a big plate with chicken** to eat,
And sometimes **ice cream** for a treat.
Blue and red are colours I like a lot,
My **doll** is the best present I ever got.
My favourite people are **Mummy, Daddy and Sophie**, who are gems,
So this, my first poem, is just for them!

Emma Turner (4)

Little Angels, Peterborough

My First Poem

My name is **Vienna** and I go to preschool,
My best friend is **Jessica**, who is really cool.
I watch **Milkshake** on TV,
Playing **with My Little Ponies** is lots of fun for me.
I just love **chippies and nuggets** to eat,
And sometimes **peaches and custard** for a treat.
Pink is a colour I like a lot,
My **My Little Ponies** are the best presents I ever got.
My favourite person is **Daddy**, who is a gem,
So this, my first poem, is just for them!

Vienna Bird (4)
Little Angels, Sittingbourne

My First Poem

My name is George and I go to preschool,
My best friend is Theo, who is really cool.
I watch PAW Patrol on TV,
Playing with Thomas is lots of fun for me.
I just love noodles to eat,
And sometimes ice cream for a treat.
Blue is a colour I like a lot,
My PAW Patrol chair is the best present
I ever got.
My favourite person is Daddy, who is a gem,
So this, my first poem, is just for them!

George Robbins (3)
Little Angels, Sittingbourne

My First Poem

My name is **Sophia** and I go to preschool,
My best friend is **Vienna**, who is really cool.
I watch **Frozen** on TV,
Playing **horses** is lots of fun for me.
I just love **baked beans** to eat,
And sometimes **chocolate cake** for a treat.
Pink is a colour I like a lot,
My **doll** is the best present I ever got.
My favourite person is **Vienna**, who is a gem,
So this, my first poem, is just for them!

Sophia Bicker (4)

Little Angels, Sittingbourne

My First Poem

My name is **Finley** and I go to preschool,
My best friend is **Logan**, who is really cool.
I watch **Marvel Avengers** on TV,
Playing **with Lego** is lots of fun for me.
I just love **shepherd's pie** to eat,
And sometimes **ice cream** for a treat.
White is a colour I like a lot,
My **Spider-Man** is the best present I ever got.
My favourite person is **Nyah**, who is a gem,
So this, my first poem, is just for them!

Finley Brunger (4)

Little Angels, Sittingbourne

My First Poem

My name is **Logan** and I go to preschool,
My best friend is **Finley**, who is really cool.
I watch **Spider-Man** on TV,
Playing **with Lego** is lots of fun for me.
I just love **crackers** to eat,
And sometimes **cake** for a treat.
Yellow is a colour I like a lot,
My **Ultimate Spider-Man** is the best present I ever got.
My favourite person is **Finley**, who is a gem,
So this, my first poem, is just for them!

Logan Hook (4)
Little Angels, Sittingbourne

My First Poem

My name is **Kourtney** and I go to preschool,
My best friend is **Sophia**, who is really cool.
I watch **films** on TV,
Playing **with Iqra** is lots of fun for me.
I just love **cookies** to eat,
And sometimes **biscuits** for a treat.
Pink is a colour I like a lot,
My **Frozen toy** is the best present I ever got.
My favourite person is **Daddy**, who is a gem,
So this, my first poem, is just for them!

Kourtney Pout (4)

Little Angels, Sittingbourne

My First Poem

My name is **Emily** and I go to preschool,
My best friend is **Jess**, who is really cool.
I watch **Peppa Pig** on TV,
Playing **with dollies** is lots of fun for me.
I just love **fish** to eat,
And sometimes **ice cream** for a treat.
Green is a colour I like a lot,
My **big doggy** is the best present I ever got.
My favourite person is **Kerry**, who is a gem,
So this, my first poem, is just for them!

Emily Corbin (3)
Little Angels, Sittingbourne

My First Poem

My name is Riley and I go to preschool,
My best friend is Ruby, who is really cool.
I watch Peppa Pig on TV,
Playing with my My Little Pony is lots of fun for me.
I just love Pot Noodle to eat,
And sometimes Happy Meal for a treat.
Blue is a colour I like a lot,
My Spider-Man is the best present I ever got.
My favourite person is Paige, who is a gem,
So this, my first poem, is just for them!

Riley Smith (4)

Little Oaks Nursery, Boston

My First Poem

My name is **Maisie** and I go to preschool,
My best friend is **Reggi**, who is really cool.
I watch **Strictly Come Dancing** on TV,
Playing **with Peppa Pig** is lots of fun for me.
I just love **chocolate** to eat,
And sometimes **sweeties** for a treat.
Blue is a colour I like a lot,
My **scooter** is the best present I ever got.
My favourite person is **Mummy**, who is a gem,
So this, my first poem, is just for them!

Maisie Pope (4)

Little Oaks Nursery, Boston

My First Poem

My name is Paige and I go to preschool,
My best friend is Chloe, who is really cool.
I watch Lego on TV,
Playing with Lego is lots of fun for me.
I just love oranges to eat,
And sometimes bananas for a treat.
Green is a colour I like a lot,
My jigsaw is the best present I ever got.
My favourite person is Mummy, who is a gem,
So this, my first poem, is just for them!

Paige Davidson (3)
Little Oaks Nursery, Boston

My First Poem

My name is **Shayla** and I go to preschool,
My best friend is **Alex**, who is really cool.
I watch **Peppa Pig** on TV,
Playing **shopkeepers** is lots of fun for me.
I just love **beans** to eat,
And sometimes **sweeties** for a treat.
Pink is a colour I like a lot,
My **robot** is the best present I ever got.
My favourite person is **Alex**, who is a gem,
So this, my first poem, is just for them!

Shayla Woods (4)
Little Oaks Nursery, Boston

My First Poem

My name is **Alex** and I go to preschool,
My best friend is **Shayla**, who is really cool.
I watch **Madagascar** on TV,
Playing **with pennies** is lots of fun for me.
I just love **sausages** to eat,
And sometimes **pizza** for a treat.
Green is a colour I like a lot,
My **teddy** is the best present I ever got.
My favourite person is **Stick Man**, who is a gem,
So this, my first poem, is just for them!

Alex Newson (3)

Little Oaks Nursery, Boston

My First Poem

My name is **Ruby** and I go to preschool,
My best friend is **Mummy**, who is really cool.
I watch **Peppa Pig** on TV,
Playing **with toys** is lots of fun for me.
I just love **toast** to eat,
And sometimes **ham** for a treat.
Orange is a colour I like a lot,
My **car** is the best present I ever got.
My favourite person is **Mummy**, who is a gem,
So this, my first poem, is just for them!

Ruby Davidson (3)

Little Oaks Nursery, Boston

My First Poem

My name is **Miley** and I go to preschool,
My best friend is **Keira**, who is really cool.
I watch **Peppa Pig** on TV,
Playing **Pie Face** is lots of fun for me.
I just love **pizza** to eat,
And sometimes **sweeties** for a treat.
Green is a colour I like a lot,
My **Frozen bike** is the best present I ever got.
My favourite person is **Ashton**, who is a gem,
So this, my first poem, is just for them!

Miley Chloe Jasmine Hancock (3)

Little Oaks Nursery, Boston

My First Poem

My name is **Lenny** and I go to preschool,
My best friend is **Reggi**, who is really cool.
I watch **Ninja Turtles** on TV,
Playing **dinosaurs** is lots of fun for me.
I just love **apples** to eat,
And sometimes **crisps** for a treat.
Blue is a colour I like a lot,
My **Hulk Buster** is the best present I ever got.
My favourite person is **Reggi**, who is a gem,
So this, my first poem, is just for them!

Lenny Teft (4)

Little Oaks Nursery, Boston

My First Poem

My name is **Taylor** and I go to preschool,
My best friend is **Andrew**, who is really cool.
I watch **Peppa Pig** on TV,
Playing **with the Hoover** is lots of fun for me.
I just love **crumpets** to eat,
And sometimes **chocolate** for a treat.
Purple is a colour I like a lot,
My **scooter** is the best present I ever got.
My favourite person is **Grandad**, who is a gem,
So this, my first poem, is just for them!

Taylor Adams (3)

Little Oaks Nursery, Boston

My First Poem

My name is **Maddison** and I go to preschool,
My best friend is **Lillie**, who is really cool.
I watch **mermaids** on TV,
Playing **dressing up** is lots of fun for me.
I just love **spaghetti on toast** to eat,
And sometimes **ice cream** for a treat.
Pink is a colour I like a lot,
My **Smarties** are the best present I ever got.
My favourite person is **Leroy**, who is a gem,
So this, my first poem, is just for them!

Maddison Messenger (3)

Little Oaks Nursery, Boston

My First Poem

My name is Reggi and I go to preschool,
My best friend is Lenny, who is really cool.
I watch One Direction on TV,
Playing Venom is lots of fun for me.
I just love chips to eat,
And sometimes sweets for a treat.
Yellow is a colour I like a lot,
My Venom Mash'em is the best present I ever got.
My favourite person is Lenny, who is a gem,
So this, my first poem, is just for them!

Reggi Vernon (4)
Little Oaks Nursery, Boston

My First Poem

My name is **Lillie** and I go to preschool,
My best friend is **Alli**, who is really cool.
I watch **Frozen** on TV,
Playing **babies** is lots of fun for me.
I just love **chicken nuggets** to eat,
And sometimes **biscuits** for a treat.
Pink is a colour I like a lot,
My **baby** is the best present I ever got.
My favourite person is **Mummy**, who is a gem,
So this, my first poem, is just for them!

Lillie Rowett (4)

Little Oaks Nursery, Boston

My First Poem

My name is **Amelia** and I go to preschool,
My best friend is **Maisie**, who is really cool.
I watch **Octonauts** on TV,
Playing **Batman** is lots of fun for me.
I just love **cake** to eat,
And sometimes **chocolate** for a treat.
White is a colour I like a lot,
My **Ninja Turtle** is the best present I ever got.
My favourite person is **Reggi**, who is a gem,
So this, my first poem, is just for them!

Amelia Grace Keal (3)

Little Oaks Nursery, Boston

My First Poem

My name is Andrew and I go to preschool,
My best friend is Taylor, who is really cool.
I watch Jurassic World on TV,
Playing with the diggers is lots of fun for me.
I just love cheese and ketchup sandwiches to eat,
And sometimes chocolate for a treat.
Green is a colour I like a lot,
My dragon is the best present I ever got.
My favourite person is Joshua, who is a gem,
So this, my first poem, is just for them!

Andrew Leyland (3)
Little Oaks Nursery, Boston

My First Poem

My name is **Emilija** and I go to preschool,
My best friend is **Arina**, who is really cool.
I watch **Frozen** on TV,
Playing **shops** is lots of fun for me.
I just love **chocolate** to eat,
And sometimes **sweets** for a treat.
Yellow is a colour I like a lot,
My **flower** is the best present I ever got.
My favourite person is **Arina**, who is a gem,
So this, my first poem, is just for them!

Emilija Rimkute (3)

Little Oaks Nursery, Boston

My First Poem

My name is Chloe and I go to preschool,
My best friend is Taylor, who is really cool.
I watch Mickey Mouse on TV,
Playing babies is lots of fun for me.
I just love cucumber to eat,
And sometimes a chocolate bar for a treat.
Red is a colour I like a lot,
My bike is the best present I ever got.
My favourite person is Nanny, who is a gem,
So this, my first poem, is just for them!

Chloe Dent (4)

Little Oaks Nursery, Boston

My First Poem

My name is **Jacob** and I go to preschool,
My best friend is **Lillie**, who is really cool.
I watch **aeroplanes** on TV,
Playing **with my toys** is lots of fun for me.
I just love **chips** to eat,
And sometimes **chocolate** for a treat.
Green is a colour I like a lot,
My **hippo game** is the best present I ever got.
My favourite person is **Callum**, who is a gem,
So this, my first poem, is just for them!

Jacob Moore (3)

Little Oaks Nursery, Boston

My First Poem

My name is **Alex** and I go to preschool,
My best friend is **Sam**, who is really cool.
I watch **Blaze** on TV,
Playing **with Fireman Sam** is lots of fun for me.
I just love **pasta** to eat,
And sometimes **spicy chicken** for a treat.
Red is a colour I like a lot,
My **boat** is the best present I ever got.
My favourite person is **Mummy**, who is a gem,
So this, my first poem, is just for them!

Alex Done (4)

Little Oaks Nursery, Boston

My First Poem

My name is Ella and I go to preschool,
My best friend is Lilly, who is really cool.
I watch Dora the Explorer on TV,
Playing with my Lego is lots of fun for me.
I just love pizza to eat,
And sometimes ice cream for a treat.
Purple is a colour I like a lot,
My microphone Elsa is the best present
I ever got.
My favourite person is Lilly, who is a gem,
So this, my first poem, is just for them!

Ella George (4)

Loughgall Playgroup, Armagh

My First Poem

My name is **Johnny** and I go to preschool,
My best friend is **Joshua**, who is really cool.
I watch **Peter Rabbit** on TV,
Playing **with my shark** is lots of fun for me.
I just love **carrot and lentil soup** to eat,
And sometimes **bonbons** for a treat.
Pink is a colour I like a lot,
My **quad** is the best present I ever got.
My favourite person is **Mummy**, who is a gem,
So this, my first poem, is just for them!

Johnny Patterson (4)

Loughgall Playgroup, Armagh

My First Poem

My name is **Farrah** and I go to preschool,
My best friend is **Ella**, who is really cool.
I watch **Tiny Paws** on TV,
Playing **with prams** is lots of fun for me.
I just love **sausages** to eat,
And sometimes **chocolate bars** for a treat.
White is a colour I like a lot,
My **bike** is the best present I ever got.
My favourite person is **Jodie**, who is a gem,
So this, my first poem, is just for them!

Farrah Forbes (3)

Loughgall Playgroup, Armagh

My First Poem

My name is Sophia and I go to preschool,
My best friend is Jodie, who is really cool.
I watch dog films on TV,
Playing with doggy monster toys is lots of fun for me.
I just love pasta to eat,
And sometimes sweets for a treat.
Pink is a colour I like a lot,
My dog is the best present I ever got.
My favourite person is Ella, who is a gem,
So this, my first poem, is just for them!

Sophia Calvin (3)
Loughgall Playgroup, Armagh

My First Poem

My name is **Jodie** and I go to preschool,
My best friend is **Sophia**, who is really cool.
I watch **Doc McStuffins** on TV,
Playing **with my toys** is lots of fun for me.
I just love **soup** to eat,
And sometimes **ice cream** for a treat.
Purple is a colour I like a lot,
My **big doll** is the best present I ever got.
My favourite person is **Ella**, who is a gem,
So this, my first poem, is just for them!

Jodie E White (4)

Loughgall Playgroup, Armagh

My First Poem

My name is Arthur and I go to preschool,
My best friend is Lucy, who is really cool.
I watch PAW Patrol and Ben & Holly on TV,
Playing tennis is lots of fun for me.
I just love tomato soup to eat,
And sometimes ice cream for a treat.
Orange is a colour I like a lot,
My Lego is the best present I ever got.
My favourite person is Mummy, who is a gem,
So this, my first poem, is just for them!

Arthur Homan (4)

Nassington Preschool, Peterborough

My First Poem

My name is **Noah** and I go to preschool,
My best friend is **Daisy**, who is really cool.
I watch **PAW Patrol and Blaze** on TV,
Playing **rockets** is lots of fun for me.
I just love **cheese sandwiches** to eat,
And sometimes **sweeties** for a treat.
Orange is a colour I like a lot,
My **remote control car and robot dog** are the best presents I ever got.
My favourite person is **Mummy**, who is a gem,
So this, my first poem, is just for them!

Noah Dorward (4)

Nassington Preschool, Peterborough

My First Poem

My name is **Daisy** and I go to preschool,
My best friend is **Noah**, who is really cool.
I watch **Frozen Fever and Beauty & the Beast** on TV,
Playing **Cupcake cards** is lots of fun for me.
I just love **fish fingers and chips** to eat,
And sometimes **chocolate bars** for a treat.
Purple is a colour I like a lot,
My **bike and dollies** are the best presents
I ever got.
My favourite person is **Daddy**, who is a gem,
So this, my first poem, is just for them!

Daisy Dorward (4)
Nassington Preschool, Peterborough

My First Poem

My name is **Lucy** and I go to preschool,
My best friend is **Arthur**, who is really cool.
I watch **Gigglebiz** on TV,
Playing **with my dogs** is lots of fun for me.
I just love **sweets** to eat,
And sometimes **cake** for a treat.
Green is a colour I like a lot,
My **Play-Doh** is the best present I ever got.
My favourite person is **Tiggy**, who is a gem,
So this, my first poem, is just for them!

Lucy Jenkinson (4)

Nassington Preschool, Peterborough

My First Poem

My name is **Lucy** and I go to preschool,
My best friend is **Lyra**, who is really cool.
I watch **Go Jetters** on TV,
Playing **with the dog** is lots of fun for me.
I just love **spaghetti** to eat,
And sometimes **sweets** for a treat.
Orange is a colour I like a lot,
My **spotty dog** is the best present I ever got.
My favourite person is **Harry**, who is a gem,
So this, my first poem, is just for them!

Lucy Earl (3)
Nassington Preschool, Peterborough

My First Poem

My name is **Matilda** and I go to preschool,
My best friend is **Alexa**, who is really cool.
I watch **Topsy and Tim** on TV,
Playing **baby schools** is lots of fun for me.
I just love **pesto pasta** to eat,
And sometimes **sweets** for a treat.
Purple and pink are colours I like a lot,
My **bike** is the best present I ever got.
My favourite person is **Balen the dog**, who is a gem,
So this, my first poem, is just for them!

Matilda Rickwood (3)

Nassington Preschool, Peterborough

My First Poem

My name is **Alfie** and I go to preschool,
My best friend is **Abrie**, who is really cool.
I watch **Mr Bean** on TV,
Playing **with Batman toys** is lots of fun for me.
I just love **chicken pops** to eat,
And sometimes **sweets** for a treat.
Blue is a colour I like a lot,
My **Batman cave** is the best present I ever got.
My favourite person is **Luna, our cat**, who is a gem,
So this, my first poem, is just for them!

Alfie Thomas (3)
Orton St Johns Preschool, Peterborough

My First Poem

My name is **Dennis** and I go to preschool,
My best friend is **Daniel**, who is really cool.
I watch **Blaze and the Monster Machines** on TV,
Playing **Mario and Luigi with Mummy** is lots of fun for me.
I just love **chow mein** to eat,
And sometimes **a Wagon Wheel** for a treat.
Red is a colour I like a lot,
My **police bike** is the best present I ever got.
My favourite person is **Daniel**, who is a gem,
So this, my first poem, is just for them!

Dennis Jack Herbert (4)

Orton St Johns Preschool, Peterborough

My First Poem

My name is **Alison** and I go to preschool,
My best friend is **Mummy**, who is really cool.
I watch **Mr Bean** on TV,
Playing **ponies** is lots of fun for me.
I just love **pizza** to eat,
And sometimes **Arctic roll** for a treat.
Pink is a colour I like a lot,
My **scooter** is the best present I ever got.
My favourite person is **Leagh**, who is a gem,
So this, my first poem, is just for them!

Alison Bradbury (3)
Orton St Johns Preschool, Peterborough

My First Poem

My name is Jamie-Leigh and I go to preschool,
My best friend is Scarlet, my sister, who is really cool.
I watch Charley Bear on TV,
Playing with my doggy is lots of fun for me.
I just love oranges to eat,
And sometimes chocolate for a treat.
Red is a colour I like a lot,
My car is the best present I ever got.
My favourite person is Scarlet, who is a gem,
So this, my first poem, is just for them!

Jamie-Leigh Cooper (2)

Orton St Johns Preschool, Peterborough

My First Poem

My name is Charlie and I go to preschool,
My best friend is Frankie, who is really cool.
I watch Topsy and Tim on TV,
Playing with my cars is lots of fun for me.
I just love juicy strawberries to eat,
And sometimes ice cream for a treat.
Green is a colour I like a lot,
My big boy bike is the best present I ever got.
My favourite person is Mummy, who is a gem,
So this, my first poem, is just for them!

Charlie Mark Uff (3)
Orton St Johns Preschool, Peterborough

My First Poem

My name is Crystal and I go to preschool,
My best friend is Cody, who is really cool.
I watch Thomas on TV,
Playing with the kitchen is lots of fun for me.
I just love toast to eat,
And sometimes chocolate buttons for a treat.
Pink is a colour I like a lot,
My bricks are the best present I ever got.
My favourite person is Mummy, who is a gem,
So this, my first poem, is just for them!

Crystal Bailey (3)
Orton St Johns Preschool, Peterborough

My First Poem

My name is Joshua and I go to preschool,
My best friends are Maddison and Jenna, who are really cool.
I watch Team Umizoomi and Cinderella on TV,
Playing with fire engines, police cars and buses with children is lots of fun for me.
I just love sausages, beans and mash to eat,
And sometimes custard for a treat.
Orange and pink are colours I like a lot,
My Peppa Pig kitchen and George bike are the best presents I ever got.
My favourite people are Mummy and Emma, who are gems,
So this, my first poem, is just for them!

Joshua Allcorn (3)

Orton St Johns Preschool, Peterborough

My First Poem

My name is **Morgan** and I go to preschool,
My best friend is **Rhianna**, who is really cool.
I watch **Peppa Pig** on TV,
Playing **football** is lots of fun for me.
I just love **chicken** to eat,
And sometimes **chocolate** for a treat.
Red is a colour I like a lot,
My **InnoTab Max** is the best present I ever got.
My favourite person is **Emma**, who is a gem,
So this, my first poem, is just for them!

Morgan Robert Glynn (3)
Orton St Johns Preschool, Peterborough

My First Poem

My name is **Dawid** and I go to preschool,
My best friend is **Karolina the teacher**, who is really cool.
I watch **Flash** on TV,
Playing **games and with Lego** is lots of fun for me.
I just love **pierogi and pancakes** to eat,
And sometimes **buns** for a treat.
Blue is a colour I like a lot,
My **McQueen car** is the best present I ever got.
My favourite person is **Kacper, my brother**, who is a gem,
So this, my first poem, is just for them!

Dawid Olszowski (3)
Orton St Johns Preschool, Peterborough

My First Poem

My name is **Harry** and I go to preschool,
My best friend is **Mummy**, who is really cool.
I watch **Blaze and the Monster Machines** on TV,
Playing **with Disney Cars and Thomas trains** is lots of fun for me.
I just love **sweeties and chocolate** to eat,
And sometimes **wobbly jelly** for a treat.
Blue is a colour I like a lot,
My **doggy, Dotty,** is the best present I ever got.
My favourite person is **Daddy**, who is a gem,
So this, my first poem, is just for them!

Harry Jacob Gray (3)
Orton St Johns Preschool, Peterborough

My First Poem

My name is **Maddie** and I go to preschool,
My best friends are **Mummy, William and Buddy**, who are really cool.
I watch **CBeebies** on TV,
Playing **babies and with the kittens** is lots of fun for me.
I just love **chicken and spaghetti** to eat,
And sometimes **a Kinder egg Surprise** for a treat.
Pink is a colour I like a lot,
My **Frozen bike and unicorn** are the best presents I ever got.
My favourite people are **Big Charlie and Little Charlie**, who are gems,
So this, my first poem, is just for them!

Maddison Louise Sinnott Brooker (3)

Orton St Johns Preschool, Peterborough

My First Poem

My name is **Shara** and I go to preschool,
My best friend is **Karla**, who is really cool.
I watch **Blaze Monster Truck** on TV,
Playing **with Shopkins** is lots of fun for me.
I just love **fish and vegetables** to eat,
And sometimes **ice cream** for a treat.
Pink is a colour I like a lot,
My **big pink kitchen** is the best present I ever got.
My favourite person is **Daddy**, who is a gem,
So this, my first poem, is just for them!

Shara Brewer (3)

Orton St Johns Preschool, Peterborough

My First Poem

My name is **George** and I go to preschool,
My best friend is **Tilly**, who is really cool.
I watch **otters** on TV,
Playing **with the tractor** is lots of fun for me.
I just love **ice cream** to eat,
And sometimes **chocolate** for a treat.
Blue is a colour I like a lot,
My **digger** is the best present I ever got.
My favourite person is **John**, who is a gem,
So this, my first poem, is just for them!

George Carnes (2)
Oulton Abbey Playgroup, Stone

My First Poem

My name is **Thomas** and I go to preschool,
My best friend is **Edmund**, who is really cool.
I watch **PAW Patrol** on TV,
Playing **with tractors** is lots of fun for me.
I just love **peas** to eat,
And sometimes **ice cream** for a treat.
Green is a colour I like a lot,
My **cattle lorry** is the best present I ever got.
My favourite person is **Tracey**, who is a gem,
So this, my first poem, is just for them!

Thomas Gadsbey (3)

Oulton Abbey Playgroup, Stone

My First Poem

My name is **Tilly** and I go to preschool,
My best friend is **Granny**, who is really cool.
I watch **Peppa Pig** on TV,
Playing **with toys** is lots of fun for me.
I just love **bananas** to eat,
And sometimes **ice cream** for a treat.
Yellow is a colour I like a lot,
My **pushchair** is the best present I ever got.
My favourite person is **Nana**, who is a gem,
So this, my first poem, is just for them!

Tilly Follwell (2)
Oulton Abbey Playgroup, Stone

My First Poem

My name is Monty and I go to preschool,
My best friend is Daddy, who is really cool.
I watch PAW Patrol on TV,
Playing with cars is lots of fun for me.
I just love fish fingers to eat,
And sometimes get Spider-Man paper for a treat.
Blue is a colour I like a lot,
My digger is the best present I ever got.
My favourite person is Daddy, who is a gem,
So this, my first poem, is just for them!

Monty Hartwell Priest (3)

Oulton Abbey Playgroup, Stone

My First Poem

My name is **Stanley** and I go to preschool,
My best friend is **Joshua**, who is really cool.
I watch **Peter Rabbit** on TV,
Playing **guiders** is lots of fun for me.
I just love **fish and chips** to eat,
And sometimes **chocolate** for a treat.
Blue and red are colours I like a lot,
My **big red combine** is the best present I ever got.
My favourite person is **Mummy**, who is a gem,
So this, my first poem, is just for them!

Stanley Roycroft (4)

Oulton Abbey Playgroup, Stone

My First Poem

My name is Annabel and I go to preschool,
My best friend is Charlotte, who is really cool.
I watch Peppa Pig on TV,
Playing with my doggy is lots of fun for me.
I just love pancakes to eat,
And sometimes ice cream for a treat.
Orange is a colour I like a lot,
My Peppa Pig microphone is the best present
I ever got.
My favourite person is Charlotte, who is a gem,
So this, my first poem, is just for them!

Annabel Rose Dickson (3)
Oulton Abbey Playgroup, Stone

My First Poem

My name is **Reuben** and I go to preschool,
My best friend is **Charlotte**, who is really cool.
I watch **Scooby-Doo Halloween** on TV,
Playing **the trumpet** is lots of fun for me.
I just love **pasties** to eat,
And sometimes **sweets** for a treat.
Orange is a colour I like a lot,
My **sea dragons** are the best present I ever got.
My favourite person is **Mummy**, who is a gem,
So this, my first poem, is just for them!

Reuben Seth Hartley Dawson (4)
Oulton Abbey Playgroup, Stone

My First Poem

My name is **Charlotte-Lucy** and I go to preschool,
My best friend is **Annabel**, who is really cool.
I watch **Peter Rabbit** on TV,
Playing **and drawing** is lots of fun for me.
I just love **biscuits and bananas** to eat,
And sometimes **chocolate** for a treat.
Pink is a colour I like a lot,
My **doll's house** is the best present I ever got.
My favourite people are **Granny, Grandma and Grandpa**, who are gems,
So this, my first poem, is just for them!

Charlotte-Lucy Ogle (3)

Oulton Abbey Playgroup, Stone

My First Poem

My name is Lillie and I go to preschool,
My best friend is Rosa, who is really cool.
I watch Peppa Pig on TV,
Playing princesses is lots of fun for me.
I just love pasta to eat,
And sometimes chocolate for a treat.
Pink is a colour I like a lot,
My Pong is the best present I ever got.
My favourite person is Rosa, who is a gem,
So this, my first poem, is just for them!

Lillie Rose Ames (3)
Oulton Abbey Playgroup, Stone

My First Poem

My name is Arthur and I go to preschool,
My best friend is Connie, who is really cool.
I watch tractor films on TV,
Playing with my tractors is lots of fun for me.
I just love grapes to eat,
And sometimes teddy bear sweets for a treat.
Blue is a colour I like a lot,
My remote control tractor is the best present I ever got.
My favourite person is Connie, who is a gem,
So this, my first poem, is just for them!

Arthur Seabridge (3)

Oulton Abbey Playgroup, Stone

My First Poem

My name is Connie and I go to preschool,
My best friend is Daddy, who is really cool.
I watch Peppa Pig on TV,
Playing with bubbles is lots of fun for me.
I just love bananas to eat,
And sometimes teddy bear sweets for a treat.
Pink is a colour I like a lot,
My pink present is the best present I ever got.
My favourite person is Daddy, who is a gem,
So this, my first poem, is just for them!

Connie Seabridge (2)

Oulton Abbey Playgroup, Stone

My First Poem

My name is Joshua and I go to preschool,
My best friend is Stanley, who is really cool.
I watch Ninja Turtles and PAW Patrol on TV,
Playing I'm the king of the castle is lots of fun for me.
I just love potatoes, carrots and meat to eat,
And sometimes jam tarts for a treat.
Green is a colour I like a lot,
My Ninja Turtle machine is the best present I ever got.
My favourite person is Mummy, who is a gem,
So this, my first poem, is just for them!

Joshua Follwell (4)
Oulton Abbey Playgroup, Stone

My First Poem

My name is **Alexie** and I go to preschool,
My best friend is **Gemma**, who is really cool.
I watch **Peppa Pig** on TV,
Playing **with dollies** is lots of fun for me.
I just love **chippies** to eat,
And sometimes **sweets** for a treat.
Pink is a colour I like a lot,
My **book** is the best present I ever got.
My favourite person is **Mummy**, who is a gem,
So this, my first poem, is just for them!

Alexie Cook (3)
Penguin Preschool, Great Yarmouth

My First Poem

My name is **Melissa** and I go to preschool,
My best friend is **Henry**, who is really cool.
I watch **Barbie** on TV,
Playing **in the kitchen** is lots of fun for me.
I just love **pasta and cheese** to eat,
And sometimes **cake** for a treat.
Pink is a colour I like a lot,
My **kitchen** is the best present I ever got.
My favourite person is **Skye**, who is a gem,
So this, my first poem, is just for them!

Melissa Griffin (4)

Penguin Preschool, Great Yarmouth

My First Poem

My name is Liara and I go to preschool,
My best friend is Connie, who is really cool.
I watch Goldilocks on TV,
Playing statues is lots of fun for me.
I just love chicken nuggets to eat,
And sometimes chocolate for a treat.
Purple is a colour I like a lot,
My teddy is the best present I ever got.
My favourite person is Elsa, who is a gem,
So this, my first poem, is just for them!

Liara McKay (4)
Penguin Preschool, Great Yarmouth

My First Poem

My name is **Lola-Rose** and I go to preschool,
My best friend is **Shyla**, who is really cool.
I watch **Cinderella** on TV,
Playing **with teddies** is lots of fun for me.
I just love **roast dinners** to eat,
And sometimes **cake** for a treat.
Pink is a colour I like a lot,
My **yo-yo** is the best present I ever got.
My favourite person is **Mummy**, who is a gem,
So this, my first poem, is just for them!

Lola-Rose Ria Savage (3)
Penguin Preschool, Great Yarmouth

My First Poem

My name is Braydon and I go to preschool,
My best friend is Jordan, who is really cool.
I watch Hulk on TV,
Playing Hulk is lots of fun for me.
I just love nuggets to eat,
And sometimes ice cream for a treat.
Green is a colour I like a lot,
My Spider-Man is the best present I ever got.
My favourite person is Jordan, who is a gem,
So this, my first poem, is just for them!

Braydon Dean Price (4)
Penguin Preschool, Great Yarmouth

My First Poem

My name is Jordan and I go to preschool,
My best friend is Stanley, who is really cool.
I watch Thomas on TV,
Playing with Thomas is lots of fun for me.
I just love sausages to eat,
And sometimes ice cream for a treat.
Orange is a colour I like a lot,
My Thomas is the best present I ever got.
My favourite person is Mummy, who is a gem,
So this, my first poem, is just for them!

Jordan Whawell (3)

Penguin Preschool, Great Yarmouth

My First Poem

My name is **Kelvin** and I go to preschool,
My best friend is **Jacob**, who is really cool.
I watch **Fireman Sam** on TV,
Playing **with Play-Doh** is lots of fun for me.
I just love **toast** to eat,
And sometimes **cake** for a treat.
Purple is a colour I like a lot,
My **Thomas the Tank** is the best present
I ever got.
My favourite person is **Mummy**, who is a gem,
So this, my first poem, is just for them!

Kelvin Williams (3)
Penguin Preschool, Great Yarmouth

My First Poem

My name is **Madison** and I go to preschool,
My best friend is **Maisie**, who is really cool.
I watch **My Little Pony** on TV,
Playing **games** is lots of fun for me.
I just love **chicken nuggets** to eat,
And sometimes **ice cream** for a treat.
Pink is a colour I like a lot,
My **books** are the best present I ever got.
My favourite person is **Mummy**, who is a gem,
So this, my first poem, is just for them!

Madison Lily Skevington (4)

Penguin Preschool, Great Yarmouth

My First Poem

My name is **Gemma** and I go to preschool,
My best friend is **Daddy**, who is really cool.
I watch **Frozen** on TV,
Playing **with teddies** is lots of fun for me.
I just love **roast dinner** to eat,
And sometimes **crisps** for a treat.
Yellow is a colour I like a lot,
My **hula hoop** is the best present I ever got.
My favourite person is **Mummy**, who is a gem,
So this, my first poem, is just for them!

Gemma Rose Townsend (3)
Penguin Preschool, Great Yarmouth

My First Poem

My name is **Olly** and I go to preschool,
My best friend is **Richard**, who is really cool.
I watch **Thomas** on TV,
Playing **with the trains** is lots of fun for me.
I just love **chicken nuggets** to eat,
And sometimes **sweets** for a treat.
Green is a colour I like a lot,
My **trains** are the best present I ever got.
My favourite person is **Mummy**, who is a gem,
So this, my first poem, is just for them!

Olly Beggs (3)
Penguin Preschool, Great Yarmouth

My First Poem

My name is **Joshua** and I go to preschool,
My best friend is **Isla**, who is really cool.
I watch **Nexo Knights** on TV,
Playing **superheroes** is lots of fun for me.
I just love **carrots** to eat,
And sometimes **a Kinder egg** for a treat.
Yellow is a colour I like a lot,
My **PAW Patrol Busy Book** is the best present
I ever got.
My favourite person is **my sister, Lilly**,
who is a gem,
So this, my first poem, is just for them!

Joshua Goldsmith (4)
Roborough Preschool, Plymouth

My First Poem

My name is **Jacob** and I go to preschool,
My best friends are **Flynn and Abi**, who are really cool.
I watch **Andy's Dinosaur Adventures and Peter Rabbit** on TV,
Playing **Barbecue Party** is lots of fun for me.
I just love **strawberries** to eat,
And sometimes **chocolate** for a treat.
Green is a colour I like a lot,
My **Barbecue Party** is the best present I ever got.
My favourite person is **Mummy**, who is a gem,
So this, my first poem, is just for them!

Jacob Bishop (3)
Roborough Preschool, Plymouth

My First Poem

My name is **George** and I go to preschool,
My best friends are **Riley, Jack and Ella**, who are really cool.
I watch **PAW Patrol** on TV,
Playing **with puzzles** is lots of fun for me.
I just love **trifle** to eat,
And sometimes **McDonald's** for a treat.
Orange is a colour I like a lot,
My **bike** is the best present I ever got.
My favourite person is **Grandad**, who is a gem,
So this, my first poem, is just for them!

George Wright (4)
Runcton Holme Preschool, King's Lynn

My First Poem

My name is **Jack** and I go to preschool,
My best friends are **George and Arabella**, who are really cool.
I watch **Minions and Andy's Dinosaur Adventures** on TV,
Playing **with Lego** is lots of fun for me.
I just love **fish fingers** to eat,
And sometimes **a chocolate teacake** for a treat.
Blue is a colour I like a lot,
My **big digger** is the best present I ever got.
My favourite people are **Ella and my daddy**,
who are gems,
So this, my first poem, is just for them!

Jack Brighton (3)
Runcton Holme Preschool, King's Lynn

My First Poem

My name is **William** and I go to preschool,
My best friend is **George**, who is really cool.
I watch **Peppa Pig** on TV,
Playing **hide-and-seek** is lots of fun for me.
I just love **pizza** to eat,
And sometimes **ice cream** for a treat.
Pink is a colour I like a lot,
My **Rosie train** is the best present I ever got.
My favourite person is **Mummy**, who is a gem,
So this, my first poem, is just for them!

William Wedd-Johnson (3)
Runcton Holme Preschool, King's Lynn

My First Poem

My name is **James** and I go to preschool,
My best friend is **Phyllis, my sister**,
who is really cool.
I watch **Toot Toot** on TV,
Playing **tractors** is lots of fun for me.
I just love **everything** to eat,
And sometimes **sweets** for a treat.
Blue is a colour I like a lot,
My **tractor** is the best present I ever got.
My favourite person is **Mummy**, who is a gem,
So this, my first poem, is just for them!

James William David Garnham (2)

Runcton Holme Preschool, King's Lynn

My First Poem

My name is **Phyllis** and I go to preschool,
My best friend is **George**, who is really cool.
I watch **Peppa Pig** on TV,
Playing **Mummies and Daddies** is lots of fun for me.
I just love **cucumber** to eat,
And sometimes **sweets** for a treat.
Pink is a colour I like a lot,
My **scooter** is the best present I ever got.
My favourite person is **Beck, my big sister**, who is a gem,
So this, my first poem, is just for them!

Phyllis Caley Garnham (3)
Runcton Holme Preschool, King's Lynn

My First Poem

My name is **Riley** and I go to preschool,
My best friends are **Lucas and Aiden**, who are really cool.
I watch **films** on TV,
Playing **Hungry Hippos** is lots of fun for me.
I just love **fruit bars** to eat,
And sometimes **chocolate** for a treat.
Red, blue and pink are colours I like a lot,
My **Batcave** is the best present I ever got.
My favourite person is **Aiden**, who is a gem,
So this, my first poem, is just for them!

Riley Weekes (4)

Salendine Nook Preschool, Huddersfield

My First Poem

My name is Olivia and I go to preschool,
My best friend is Jorja, who is really cool.
I watch Peppa Pig on TV,
Playing with Lego is lots of fun for me.
I just love yoghurts to eat,
And sometimes sweeties and chocolate for a treat.
Yellow is a colour I like a lot,
My doll is the best present I ever got.
My favourite person is Mummy, who is a gem,
So this, my first poem, is just for them!

Olivia Margrave (2)
Salendine Nook Preschool, Huddersfield

My First Poem

My name is Elijah and I go to preschool,
My best friends are my dad and grandma, who are really cool.
I watch Spider-Man on TV,
Playing on the PlayStation is lots of fun for me.
I just love noodles to eat,
And sometimes sweets for a treat.
Blue and red are colours I like a lot,
My new Lego game and comics are the best presents I ever got.
My favourite person is Grandma, who is a gem,
So this, my first poem, is just for them!

Elijah Hall (4)
Salendine Nook Preschool, Huddersfield

My First Poem

My name is **Ava** and I go to preschool,
My best friends are **Amara and Joey**, who are really cool.
I watch **Frozen** on TV,
Playing **with my toy baby** is lots of fun for me.
I just love **grapes** to eat,
And sometimes **chocolate** for a treat.
Yellow is a colour I like a lot,
My **Kindle** is the best present I ever got.
My favourite person is **Titchy**, who is a gem,
So this, my first poem, is just for them!

Ava McCafferty (3)
Salendine Nook Preschool, Huddersfield

My First Poem

My name is Rimshah and I go to preschool,
My best friend is Ava, who is really cool.
I watch My Little Pony on TV,
Playing with ponies is lots of fun for me.
I just love carrots to eat,
And sometimes I eat chocolate for a treat.
White is a colour I like a lot,
My Frozen doll is the best present I ever got.
My favourite person is Falak, who is a gem,
So this, my first poem, is just for them!

Rimshah Shafi (4)

Salendine Nook Preschool, Huddersfield

My First Poem

My name is Jorja and I go to preschool,
My best friend is Faith, who is really cool.
I watch Frozen on TV,
Playing with Lego is lots of fun for me.
I just love cheese sandwiches to eat,
And sometimes Mini Cheddars and yoghurt for a treat.
Pink is a colour I like a lot,
My Animagic is the best present I ever got.
My favourite person is Olivia, my cousin, who is a gem,
So this, my first poem, is just for them!

Jorja Leah Lister (4)
Salendine Nook Preschool, Huddersfield

My First Poem

My name is Jonah and I go to preschool,
My best friend is Aayan, who is really cool.
I watch Power Rangers on TV,
Playing superheroes is lots of fun for me.
I just love pasta to eat,
And sometimes a chocolate egg for a treat.
Blue is a colour I like a lot,
My Transformers are the best present I ever got.
My favourite person is Leo, who is a gem,
So this, my first poem, is just for them!

Jonah Quinn (4)
Salendine Nook Preschool, Huddersfield

My First Poem

My name is **Joey** and I go to preschool,
My best friend is **Amara**, who is really cool.
I watch **Spider-Man** on TV,
Playing **with cars** is lots of fun for me.
I just love **toast** to eat,
And sometimes **chocolate** for a treat.
Blue is a colour I like a lot,
My **Ninja Turtle** is the best present I ever got.
My favourite person is **my mummy**, who is a gem,
So this, my first poem, is just for them!

Joey Thwaites (4)
Salendine Nook Preschool, Huddersfield

My First Poem

My name is **Kaleb** and I go to preschool,
My best friend is **James**, who is really cool.
I watch **Minnie Mouse, Peppa Pig and PAW Patrol** on TV,
Playing **with balloons, jigsaws and trains** is lots of fun for me.
I just love **cheese, egg, chocolate, pizza and pasta** to eat,
And sometimes **cake and sweets** for a treat.
Blue is a colour I like a lot,
My **Hulk and bag** are the best presents I ever got.
My favourite person is **Nana**, who is a gem,
So this, my first poem, is just for them!

Kaleb Wykes (4)
Salendine Nook Preschool, Huddersfield

My First Poem

My name is **Kianne** and I go to preschool,
My best friend is **mummy**, who is really cool.
I watch **Peppa Pig** on TV,
Playing **with the water and outside** is lots of fun for me.
I just love **banana and yoghurts** to eat,
And sometimes **chocolate** for a treat.
Red is a colour I like a lot,
My **balloon** is the best present I ever got.
My favourite person is **me**, who is a gem,
So this, my first poem, is just for them!

Kianne Wykes (2)
Salendine Nook Preschool, Huddersfield

My First Poem

My name is **Nathan** and I go to preschool,
My best friend is **Georgia**, who is really cool.
I watch **Thunderbirds** on TV,
Playing **with Tayo the bus** is lots of fun for me.
I just love **chicken** to eat,
And sometimes **sweets and chocolate eggs** for a treat.
Red, orange and green are colours I like a lot,
My **Thunderbirds and Tayo Bus** are the best presents I ever got.
My favourite person is **Isobella**, who is a gem,
So this, my first poem, is just for them!

Nathan Blakemore (4)
Salendine Nook Preschool, Huddersfield

My First Poem

My name is **Olivia** and I go to preschool,
My best friend is **Sophia**, who is really cool.
I watch **Blaze and the Monster Machines** on TV,
Playing **with Sophia** is lots of fun for me.
I just love **apples** to eat,
And sometimes **crisps** for a treat.
Pink is a colour I like a lot,
My **bracelet** is the best present I ever got.
My favourite person is **Sophia**, who is a gem,
So this, my first poem, is just for them!

Olivia Rose Mellor (3)

Salendine Nook Preschool, Huddersfield

My First Poem

My name is **Leo** and I go to preschool,
My best friend is **James**, who is really cool.
I watch **CBeebies** on TV,
Playing **jigsaws** is lots of fun for me.
I just love **bananas** to eat,
And sometimes **Kinder Joy** for a treat.
Red is a colour I like a lot,
My **Toy Story DVDs** is the best present I ever got.
My favourite person is **Mummy**, who is a gem,
So this, my first poem, is just for them!

Leo James Smith (3)

Salendine Nook Preschool, Huddersfield

My First Poem

My name is **Aayan** and I go to preschool,
My best friend is **Jonah**, who is really cool.
I watch **Spider-Man** on TV,
Playing **pretend Spider-Man** is lots of fun for me.
I just love **fish fingers and black lentils** to eat,
And sometimes **chocolate** for a treat.
Blue is a colour I like a lot,
My **shark toy** is the best present I ever got.
My favourite person is **my dad**, who is a gem,
So this, my first poem, is just for them!

Aayan Khaliq Uddin (3)
Salendine Nook Preschool, Huddersfield

My First Poem

My name is **Alfie** and I go to preschool,
My best friend is **Logan**, who is really cool.
I watch **Toy Story** on TV,
Playing **with cars** is lots of fun for me.
I just love **pizza** to eat,
And sometimes **chocolate** for a treat.
Yellow is a colour I like a lot,
My **Buzz dress-up** is the best present I ever got.
My favourite person is **Tracy**, who is a gem,
So this, my first poem, is just for them!

Alfie Leach (2)
Salendine Nook Preschool, Huddersfield

My First Poem

My name is **Billy** and I go to preschool,
My best friend is **Daddy**, who is really cool.
I watch **PAW Patrol** on TV,
Playing **Dinosaur Adventures** is lots of fun for me.
I just love **fish fingers** to eat,
And sometimes **a Fudge** for a treat.
Orange is a colour I like a lot,
My **John Deere tractor** is the best present I ever got.
My favourite person is **Elsie**, who is a gem,
So this, my first poem, is just for them!

Billy Broster (2)
Salendine Nook Preschool, Huddersfield

My First Poem

My name is **Asma** and I go to preschool,
My best friend is **Zara**, who is really cool.
I watch **Frozen** on TV,
Playing **princesses** is lots of fun for me.
I just love **pears** to eat,
And sometimes **chocolate** for a treat.
Purple is a colour I like a lot,
My **Barbie doll** is the best present I ever got.
My favourite person is **Mummy**, who is a gem,
So this, my first poem, is just for them!

Asma Ahmed (4)

Shining Stars Preschool Nursery, Peterborough

My First Poem

My name is Sara and I go to preschool,
My best friend is Mummy, who is really cool.
I watch Frozen on TV,
Playing and colouring is lots of fun for me.
I just love cornflakes to eat,
And sometimes chocolate for a treat.
Pink is a colour I like a lot,
My puzzle is the best present I ever got.
My favourite person is Daddy, who is a gem,
So this, my first poem, is just for them!

Sara Yasin (3)
Shining Stars Preschool Nursery, Peterborough

My First Poem

My name is **Amelia** and I go to preschool,
My best friend is **Amy**, who is really cool.
I watch **Strawberry Shortcake** on TV,
Playing **and colouring** is lots of fun for me.
I just love **fish fingers and beans** to eat,
And sometimes **cake** for a treat.
Pink is a colour I like a lot,
My **porcupine** is the best present I ever got.
My favourite person is **Amy**, who is a gem,
So this, my first poem, is just for them!

Amelia Ul-Haq (4)

Shining Stars Preschool Nursery, Peterborough

My First Poem

My name is Asad and I go to preschool,
My best friend is Amaya, who is really cool.
I watch Spider-Man on TV,
Playing with cars is lots of fun for me.
I just love pizza to eat,
And sometimes lollipops for a treat.
Orange is a colour I like a lot,
My car is the best present I ever got.
My favourite person is Amaya, who is a gem,
So this, my first poem, is just for them!

Asad Rashid (4)

Shining Stars Preschool Nursery, Peterborough

My First Poem

My name is **Lacey-Jaie** and I go to preschool,
My best friend is **Emily**, who is really cool.
I watch **Ben and Holly** on TV,
Playing **with my purple ball** is lots of fun for me.
I just love **cheese on toast** to eat,
And sometimes **lollipops** for a treat.
Pink and yellow are colours I like a lot,
My **bike** is the best present I ever got.
My favourite person is **Harper**, who is a gem,
So this, my first poem, is just for them!

Lacey-Jaie Burridge (4)
South Brent Preschool, South Brent

My First Poem

My name is **Amelia** and I go to preschool,
My best friend is **Lacey-Jaie**, who is really cool.
I watch **Ben and Holly** on TV,
Playing **with toys** is lots of fun for me.
I just love **sandwiches with cheese in** to eat,
And sometimes **sweeties** for a treat.
Pink is a colour I like a lot,
My **monkey toy** is the best present I ever got.
My favourite person is **Daddy**, who is a gem,
So this, my first poem, is just for them!

Amelia Herriott (3)
South Brent Preschool, South Brent

My First Poem

My name is Lilah and I go to preschool,
My best friend is Mummy, who is really cool.
I watch Shaun the Sheep on TV,
Playing horses is lots of fun for me.
I just love potatoes and spaghetti to eat,
And sometimes Appletiser for a treat.
Pink and white are colours I like a lot,
My pink bike with a basket is the best present
I ever got.
My favourite person is Nanny, who is a gem,
So this, my first poem, is just for them!

Lilah Schaefer (3)

South Brent Preschool, South Brent

My First Poem

My name is **Ella** and I go to preschool,
My best friend is **Elsa**, who is really cool.
I watch **Ben and Holly** on TV,
Playing **with my cousin, Teyla,** is lots of fun for me.
I just love **ham sandwiches** to eat,
And sometimes **sweets** for a treat.
Yellow and pink are colours I like a lot,
My **bike** is the best present I ever got.
My favourite people are **Mummy and Daddy,** who are gems,
So this, my first poem, is just for them!

Ella Rose Lane (2)
South Brent Preschool, South Brent

My First Poem

My name is **Evelyn** and I go to preschool,
My best friend is **Elsa**, who is really cool.
I watch **Minions** on TV,
Playing **with my Elsa doll** is lots of fun for me.
I just love **chicken and potato** to eat,
And sometimes **chocolate mousse** for a treat.
Pink is a colour I like a lot,
My **Elsa wand** is the best present I ever got.
My favourite person is **Esme**, who is a gem,
So this, my first poem, is just for them!

Evelyn Scott (3)

South Brent Preschool, South Brent

My First Poem

My name is Jack and I go to preschool,
My best friend is Max, who is really cool.
I watch Peppa Pig and Mickey Mouse on TV,
Playing with tractors and trailers is lots of fun for me.
I just love carrots and beans to eat,
And sometimes lollipops for a treat.
Red is a colour I like a lot,
My tractor is the best present I ever got.
My favourite people are Mummy and Daddy, who are gems,
So this, my first poem, is just for them!

Jack Jellicoe (3)
South Brent Preschool, South Brent

My First Poem

My name is Lacey and I go to preschool,
My best friend is Elsa, who is really cool.
I watch Cinderella on TV,
Playing with Frozen dolls is lots of fun for me.
I just love pasta and sauce to eat,
And sometimes chocolate for a treat.
Purple is a colour I like a lot,
My Frozen clothes are the best present I ever got.
My favourite person is Whitney, who is a gem,
So this, my first poem, is just for them!

Lacey Davies (4)
South Brent Preschool, South Brent

My First Poem

My name is **Kaitlyn** and I go to preschool,
My best friends are **Mummy and Daddy**, who are really cool.
I watch **Frozen** on TV,
Playing **with dollies** is lots of fun for me.
I just love **waffles** to eat,
And sometimes **fruit** for a treat.
Pink and purple are colours I like a lot,
My **fairy wand** is the best present I ever got.
My favourite people are **Mummy and Daddy**, who are gems,
So this, my first poem, is just for them!

Kaitlyn Hayter (3)
South Brent Preschool, South Brent

My First Poem

My name is **Reece** and I go to preschool,
My best friend is **Ruby**, who is really cool.
I watch **CBeebies and Mr Tumble** on TV,
Playing **with cars and shops** is lots of fun for me.
I just love **salad and Mexican chicken** to eat,
And sometimes **ice cream and chocolate sauce** for a treat.
Green is a colour I like a lot,
My **Scooby-Doo Mystery Machine** is the best present I ever got.
My favourite person is **my mummy**, who is a gem,
So this, my first poem, is just for them!

Reece Cook (4)

Steeple Claydon Nursery, Buckingham

My First Poem

My name is **Aston** and I go to preschool,
My best friend is **Lily**, who is really cool.
I watch **Thunderbirds** on TV,
Playing **Thunderbirds** is lots of fun for me.
I just love **chicken nuggets** to eat,
And sometimes **sweeties** for a treat.
Red is a colour I like a lot,
My **Tracy Island** is the best present I ever got.
My favourite person is **Mummy**, who is a gem,
So this, my first poem, is just for them!

Aston Field (2)

Steeple Claydon Nursery, Buckingham

My First Poem

My name is **Kai** and I go to preschool,
My best friend is **Daddy**, who is really cool.
I watch **PAW Patrol** on TV,
Playing **Crossy Road** is lots of fun for me.
I just love **tuna** to eat,
And sometimes **more tuna** for a treat.
Red is a colour I like a lot,
My **Toot Toot Drivers** is the best present
I ever got.
My favourite person is **Mummy**, who is a gem,
So this, my first poem, is just for them!

Kai Piosek-Smith (2)

Steeple Claydon Nursery, Buckingham

My First Poem

My name is **Evan** and I go to preschool,
My best friends are **Mylo and Brennan**, who are really cool.
I watch **PAW Patrol and Thomas** on TV,
Playing **with cars and PAW Patrol** is lots of fun for me.
I just love **grapes and pears** to eat,
And sometimes **chocolate** for a treat.
Red is a colour I like a lot,
My **PAW Patroller** is the best present I ever got.
My favourite people are **Mummy, Daddy and Oscar**, who are gems,
So this, my first poem, is just for them!

Evan Timothy Wedley (4)
Steeple Claydon Nursery, Buckingham

My First Poem

My name is **Brennan** and I go to preschool,
My best friend is **Mylo**, who is really cool.
I watch **Mickey Mouse** on TV,
Playing **superheroes** is lots of fun for me.
I just love **pepperoni** to eat,
And sometimes **a chocolate egg** for a treat.
Yellow is a colour I like a lot,
My **Woody** is the best present I ever got.
My favourite person is **Mylo**, who is a gem,
So this, my first poem, is just for them!

Brennan Michael Donald Lee (3)

Steeple Claydon Nursery, Buckingham

My First Poem

My name is **Jamie** and I go to preschool,
My best friend is **Freddie**, who is really cool.
I watch **Bob the Builder** on TV,
Playing **in the garden** is lots of fun for me.
I just love **apples** to eat,
And sometimes **chocolate** for a treat.
Blue is a colour I like a lot,
My **fire truck** is the best present I ever got.
My favourite person is **Mummy**, who is a gem,
So this, my first poem, is just for them!

Jamie Mills-Baughan (2)
Steeple Claydon Nursery, Buckingham

My First Poem

My name is **Kaylee** and I go to preschool,
My best friend is **Oliver**, who is really cool.
I watch **PAW Patrol** on TV,
Playing **babies** is lots of fun for me.
I just love **nuggets and chips** to eat,
And sometimes **sweets** for a treat.
Purple is a colour I like a lot,
My **PAW Patrol toys** are the best present
I ever got.
My favourite people are **Mummy and Daddy**, who are gems,
So this, my first poem, is just for them!

Kaylee Ann Paxton (4)
Steeple Claydon Nursery, Buckingham

My First Poem

My name is **Annabelle** and I go to preschool,
My best friend is **Maisy**, who is really cool.
I watch **Peppa Pig** on TV,
Playing **at the park** is lots of fun for me.
I just love **cheesy peas** to eat,
And sometimes **chocolate** for a treat.
Blue is a colour I like a lot,
My **rocket** is the best present I ever got.
My favourite person is **my mummy**, who is a gem,
So this, my first poem, is just for them!

Annabelle Gould (2)
Steeple Claydon Nursery, Buckingham

My First Poem

My name is **Harry** and I go to preschool,
My best friend is **Jacob**, who is really cool.
I watch **Thomas** on TV,
Playing **with Gordon** is lots of fun for me.
I just love **chocolate bars** to eat,
And sometimes **apples** for a treat.
Blue is a colour I like a lot,
My **Gordon** is the best present I ever got.
My favourite person is **Daddy**, who is a gem,
So this, my first poem, is just for them!

Harry Carroll (3)

Steeple Claydon Nursery, Buckingham

My First Poem

My name is Oliver and I go to preschool,
My best friend is Lucas, who is really cool.
I watch Mr Tumble on TV,
Playing with water is lots of fun for me.
I just love pasta and pizza to eat,
And sometimes ice cream for a treat.
Blue is a colour I like a lot,
My frog is the best present I ever got.
My favourite person is Lucia, who is a gem,
So this, my first poem, is just for them!

Oliver Matthias (4)
Steeple Claydon Nursery, Buckingham

My First Poem

My name is Jacob and I go to preschool,
My best friend is Harry, who is really cool.
I watch CBeebies on TV,
Playing with dinosaurs is lots of fun for me.
I just love pizza to eat,
And sometimes a lolly for a treat.
Green is a colour I like a lot,
My big dinosaur is the best present I ever got.
My favourite person is Mummy, who is a gem,
So this, my first poem, is just for them!

Jacob Butler (3)

Steeple Claydon Nursery, Buckingham

My First Poem

My name is Rosie and I go to preschool,
My best friend is Isla, who is really cool.
I watch Topsy and Tim on TV,
Playing tea shops is lots of fun for me.
I just love sausage rolls to eat,
And sometimes biscuits for a treat.
Pink is a colour I like a lot,
My scooter is the best present I ever got.
My favourite person is Auntie Kelly, who is a gem,
So this, my first poem, is just for them!

Rosie Joy Fenables (3)
Steeple Claydon Nursery, Buckingham

My First Poem

My name is **Bailey** and I go to preschool,
My best friend is **Ben**, who is really cool.
I watch **Monsters Inc** on TV,
Playing **with cars** is lots of fun for me.
I just love **apples** to eat,
And sometimes **sweets** for a treat.
Green is a colour I like a lot,
My **Spider-Man toy** is the best present I ever got.
My favourite person is **Mummy**, who is a gem,
So this, my first poem, is just for them!

Bailey Coterill (3)
The Links Nursery, Stockton-On-Tees

My First Poem

My name is **Phebe** and I go to preschool,
My best friend is **Sorcha**, who is really cool.
I watch **Alphablocks** on TV,
Playing **with toy dinosaurs** is lots of fun for me.
I just love **toast** to eat,
And sometimes **chocolate hoops** for a treat.
Pink is a colour I like a lot,
My **ice cream maker** is the best present
I ever got.
My favourite person is **Mummy**, who is a gem,
So this, my first poem, is just for them!

Phebe Crockett (4)
The Links Nursery, Stockton-On-Tees

My First Poem

My name is Sorcha and I go to preschool,
My best friend is Grandma, who is really cool.
I watch Peppa Pig on TV,
Playing football is lots of fun for me.
I just love chicken goujons to eat,
And sometimes chocolate for a treat.
Pink is a colour I like a lot,
My Christmas book is the best present I ever got.
My favourite person is Grandma, who is a gem,
So this, my first poem, is just for them!

Sorcha Bond (4)
The Links Nursery, Stockton-On-Tees

My First Poem

My name is Oliver and I go to preschool,
My best friend is Joseph, who is really cool.
I watch Spider-Man on TV,
Playing with cars is lots of fun for me.
I just love Spider-Man pasta to eat,
And sometimes Blue Ribbons for a treat.
Red is a colour I like a lot,
My Spider-Man car is the best present I ever got.
My favourite person is Joseph, who is a gem,
So this, my first poem, is just for them!

Oliver Daly (4)
The Links Nursery, Stockton-On-Tees

My First Poem

My name is **Joseph** and I go to preschool,
My best friend is **Oliver**, who is really cool.
I watch **Go Jetters** on TV,
Playing **with trains** is lots of fun for me.
I just love **pasta** to eat,
And sometimes **jelly snakes** for a treat.
Black is a colour I like a lot,
My **Marble Run** is the best present I ever got.
My favourite person is **Oliver**, who is a gem,
So this, my first poem, is just for them!

Joseph Horlock (3)
The Links Nursery, Stockton-On-Tees

My First Poem

My name is **Ted** and I go to preschool,
My best friend is **Joseph**, who is really cool.
I watch **Bob the Builder** on TV,
Playing **with my tractors** is lots of fun for me.
I just love **beans on toast** to eat,
And sometimes **chocolate biscuits** for a treat.
Orange is a colour I like a lot,
My **lawnmower** is the best present I ever got.
My favourite person is **Joseph**, who is a gem,
So this, my first poem, is just for them!

Ted Cartman (3)
The Links Nursery, Stockton-On-Tees

My First Poem

My name is **Alexander** and I go to preschool,
My best friend is **Sorcha**, who is really cool.
I watch **Go Jetters** on TV,
Playing **with my cars** is lots of fun for me.
I just love **chicken** to eat,
And sometimes **chocolate coins** for a treat.
Red is a colour I like a lot,
My **chocolate Santa** is the best present
I ever got.
My favourite person is **Tommy**, who is a gem,
So this, my first poem, is just for them!

Alexander Owen Pindor (3)
The Links Nursery, Stockton-On-Tees

My First Poem

My name is Jamie and I go to preschool,
My best friend is Jake, who is really cool.
I watch Thomas the Tank Engine on TV,
Playing with cars is lots of fun for me.
I just love pears to eat,
And sometimes chocolate for a treat.
Blue is a colour I like a lot,
My kitchen is the best present I ever got.
My favourite person is Mummy, who is a gem,
So this, my first poem, is just for them!

Jamie Carter (3)
The Links Nursery, Stockton-On-Tees

My First Poem

My name is Finnan and I go to preschool,
My best friend is Oliver, who is really cool.
I watch Spider-Man on TV,
Playing with my cars is lots of fun for me.
I just love ravioli to eat,
And sometimes sweets for a treat.
Orange is a colour I like a lot,
My pogo stick is the best present I ever got.
My favourite person is Daddy, who is a gem,
So this, my first poem, is just for them!

Finnan Brian Hanrahan (4)

The Links Nursery, Stockton-On-Tees

My First Poem

My name is **Evie** and I go to preschool,
My best friend is **Ava**, who is really cool.
I watch **Peppa Pig** on TV,
Playing **with my paint set** is lots of fun for me.
I just love **carrots** to eat,
And sometimes **sweets** for a treat.
Purple is a colour I like a lot,
My **doll** is the best present I ever got.
My favourite person is **Daddy**, who is a gem,
So this, my first poem, is just for them!

Evie Jessica Peters (3)
The Links Nursery, Stockton-On-Tees

My First Poem

My name is **Ava** and I go to preschool,
My best friend is **Evie**, who is really cool.
I watch **Peppa Pig** on TV,
Playing **with dolls** is lots of fun for me.
I just love **spaghetti** to eat,
And sometimes **chocolate** for a treat.
Brown is a colour I like a lot,
My **dance dolls** are the best present I ever got.
My favourite person is **Mummy**, who is a gem,
So this, my first poem, is just for them!

Ava Corner (4)

The Links Nursery, Stockton-On-Tees

My First Poem

My name is **Emelia** and I go to preschool,
My best friend is **Ava**, who is really cool.
I watch **Peppa Pig** on TV,
Playing **with Minnie Mouse toys** is lots of fun for me.
I just love **pizza** to eat,
And sometimes **ice cream** for a treat.
Purple is a colour I like a lot,
My **bike** is the best present I ever got.
My favourite people are **Mummy and Daddy**, who are gems,
So this, my first poem, is just for them!

Emelia Wray (3)
The Links Nursery, Stockton-On-Tees

My First Poem

My name is **Max** and I go to preschool,
My best friend is **Kalina**, who is really cool.
I watch **Fire & Rescue and Cars 2** on TV,
Playing **with cars and planes** is lots of fun for me.
I just love **pasta, cheese and meatballs** to eat,
And sometimes **Kinder eggs and chocolate** for a treat.
Orange and red are colours I like a lot,
My **Lightning McQueen** is the best present I ever got.
My favourite people are **Mummy, Daddy and Molly**, who are gems,
So this, my first poem, is just for them!

Max William Alan Foster (3)
The Willows, Didcot

My First Poem

My name is **Indie** and I go to preschool,
My best friend is **Bella**, who is really cool.
I watch **PAW Patrol** on TV,
Playing **with my tea set** is lots of fun for me.
I just love **mushrooms** to eat,
And sometimes **I get a toy** for a treat.
Pink and purple are colours I like a lot,
My **dog who walks and talks** is the best present I ever got.
My favourite person is **my mum**, who is a gem,
So this, my first poem, is just for them!

Indiana Jay Bennett (3)
The Willows, Didcot

My First Poem

My name is **Kalina** and I go to preschool,
My best friend is **Isabella**, who is really cool.
I watch **Polly Pocket** on TV,
Playing **with cars** is lots of fun for me.
I just love **strawberries and apples** to eat,
And sometimes **chocolate** for a treat.
Blue is a colour I like a lot,
My **Frozen scooter** is the best present I ever got.
My favourite people are **Mummy, Daddy, Pola and the cat too**, who are gems,
So this, my first poem, is just for them!

Kalina Kantyka (3)
The Willows, Didcot

My First Poem

My name is **Ffion** and I go to preschool,
My best friend is **Lauren**, who is really cool.
I watch **Wreck-It Ralph** on TV,
Playing **with the kitchen** is lots of fun for me.
I just love **sausages** to eat,
And sometimes **Jammy Dodger biscuits** for a treat.
Purple is a colour I like a lot,
My **pink trainers** are the best present I ever got.
My favourite person is **Oscar**, who is a gem,
So this, my first poem, is just for them!

Ffion Blundell (3)
The Willows, Didcot

My First Poem

My name is **Lauren** and I go to preschool,
My best friends are **Ffion and Pippa**, who are really cool.
I watch **Peppa Pig and Ben & Holly** on TV,
Playing **with babies and blocks** is lots of fun for me.
I just love **crunchy nuts, nuggets and chips** to eat,
And sometimes **strawberries, blueberries and chocolate squares** for a treat.
Orange, pink and red are colours I like a lot,
My **teddy** is the best present I ever got.
My favourite person is **Daddy**, who is a gem,
So this, my first poem, is just for them!

Lauren Grace (3)
The Willows, Didcot

My First Poem

My name is **Harry** and I go to preschool,
My best friend is **Cara**, who is really cool.
I watch **Peppa Pig** on TV,
Playing **with cars** is lots of fun for me.
I just love **rice and pasta** to eat,
And sometimes **sweets** for a treat.
Orange is a colour I like a lot,
My **scooter** is the best present I ever got.
My favourite person is **Mummy**, who is a gem,
So this, my first poem, is just for them!

Harry Austin (3)
The Willows, Didcot

My First Poem

My name is Ava and I go to preschool,
My best friend is Isabelle, who is really cool.
I watch Peppa Pig on TV,
Playing babies is lots of fun for me.
I just love chicken to eat,
And sometimes biscuits for a treat.
Yellow is a colour I like a lot,
My kitchen is the best present I ever got.
My favourite person is Mummy, who is a gem,
So this, my first poem, is just for them!

Ava Butler (3)
The Willows, Didcot

My First Poem

My name is **Pippa** and I go to preschool,
My best friend is **Jasmiina**, who is really cool.
I watch **Peppa Pig and PAW Patrol** on TV,
Playing **with dolls and Play-Doh** is lots of fun for me.
I just love **broccoli and salmon** to eat,
And sometimes **chocolate and ice cream** for a treat.
Pink is a colour I like a lot,
My **PAW Patrol teddy, Chase,** is the best present I ever got.
My favourite person is **Jasmiina**, who is a gem,
So this, my first poem, is just for them!

Pippa McGibbon (3)
The Willows, Didcot

My First Poem

My name is Jasmiina and I go to preschool,
My best friend is Pippa, who is really cool.
I watch Peppa Pig on TV,
Playing with Elsa and dolls is lots of fun for me.
I just love bread and cheese to eat,
And sometimes chocolate for a treat.
Pink is a colour I like a lot,
My books are the best present I ever got.
My favourite person is Pippa, who is a gem,
So this, my first poem, is just for them!

Jasmiina Alhaddad (3)

The Willows, Didcot

My First Poem

My name is **Jack** and I go to preschool,
My best friends are **Riley and Teegan**, who are really cool.
I watch **Netflix** on TV,
Playing **with trolls** is lots of fun for me.
I just love **pizza** to eat,
And sometimes **chocolate** for a treat.
Red is a colour I like a lot,
My **dinosaur** is the best present I ever got.
My favourite people are **Mummy and Grandad**, who are gems,
So this, my first poem, is just for them!

Jack Bolton (3)
The Willows, Didcot

My First Poem

My name is **Isabella** and I go to preschool,
My best friend is **Noah**, who is really cool.
I watch **Peppa Pig** on TV,
Playing **with my Frozen toys** is lots of fun for me.
I just love **sweeties** to eat,
And sometimes **chocolate** for a treat.
Pink is a colour I like a lot,
My **Elsa doll** is the best present I ever got.
My favourite person is **Noah**, who is a gem,
So this, my first poem, is just for them!

Isabella Burchell (3)

The Willows, Didcot

My First Poem

My name is **Milä** and I go to preschool,
My best friend is **Indie**, who is really cool.
I watch **Peppa Pig** on TV,
Playing **with my unicorns** is lots of fun for me.
I just love **cucumber** to eat,
And sometimes **biscuits** for a treat.
Pink is a colour I like a lot,
My **Frozen microphone** is the best present
I ever got.
My favourite person is **Mummy**, who is a gem,
So this, my first poem, is just for them!

Milä Antonia Jennifer Woods (3)
The Willows, Didcot

My First Poem

My name is Charlie and I go to preschool,
My best friend is Max, who is really cool.
I watch Fireman Sam on TV,
Playing with my tractor is lots of fun for me.
I just love pasta to eat,
And sometimes sweeties for a treat.
Pink is a colour I like a lot,
My new crayons and paper are the best presents I ever got.
My favourite person is James, who is a gem,
So this, my first poem, is just for them!

Charlie Owen (3)

The Willows, Didcot

My First Poem

My name is Cara and I go to preschool,
My best friend is Harry, who is really cool.
I watch PAW Patrol on TV,
Playing with dollies is lots of fun for me.
I just love burgers to eat,
And sometimes banana for a treat.
Blue is a colour I like a lot,
My PAW Patrol backpack is the best present I ever got.
My favourite person is Mummy, who is a gem,
So this, my first poem, is just for them!

Cara Duffy (3)
The Willows, Didcot

My First Poem

My name is Annabel and I go to preschool,
My best friend is Pippa, who is really cool.
I watch Peppa Pig on TV,
Playing with dolls is lots of fun for me.
I just love sausages to eat,
And sometimes crisps for a treat.
Red is a colour I like a lot,
My Barbie doll is the best present I ever got.
My favourite person is Sophie, who is a gem,
So this, my first poem, is just for them!

Annabel Thompson (3)

Tiny Tots Corner Playgroup, Armagh

My First Poem

My name is Myah and I go to preschool,
My best friend is Samuel, who is really cool.
I watch Peppa Pig on TV,
Playing with my microphone is lots of fun for me.
I just love chips and sausages to eat,
And sometimes sweets for a treat.
Pink is a colour I like a lot,
My Play-Doh is the best present I ever got.
My favourite people are Mummy and Daddy, who are gems,
So this, my first poem, is just for them!

Myah Sarah Morrison (4)
Tiny Tots Corner Playgroup, Armagh

My First Poem

My name is **Isaac** and I go to preschool,
My best friend is **Charlie**, who is really cool.
I watch **Laura who does silly things** on TV,
Playing **with my cow shed** is lots of fun for me.
I just love **sausages** to eat,
And sometimes **chocolate** for a treat.
Red is a colour I like a lot,
My **till** is the best present I ever got.
My favourite person is **Mummy**, who is a gem,
So this, my first poem, is just for them!

Isaac Gardiner (4)

Tiny Tots Corner Playgroup, Armagh

My First Poem

My name is **Pippa** and I go to preschool,
My best friend is **Bella**, who is really cool.
I watch **Matilda** on TV,
Playing **hide-and-seek** is lots of fun for me.
I just love **chicken nuggets** to eat,
And sometimes **sweets** for a treat.
Pink is a colour I like a lot,
My **bike** is the best present I ever got.
My favourite person is **Ollie**, who is a gem,
So this, my first poem, is just for them!

Pippa Watson (3)

Tiny Tots Corner Playgroup, Armagh

My First Poem

My name is **Jenny** and I go to preschool,
My best friend is **Anna**, who is really cool.
I watch **Peppa Pig** on TV,
Playing **with my tea set** is lots of fun for me.
I just love **sandwiches** to eat,
And sometimes **crackers** for a treat.
Pink is a colour I like a lot,
My **microphone** is the best present I ever got.
My favourite person is **Jamie**, who is a gem,
So this, my first poem, is just for them!

Jenny Agnew (4)
Tiny Tots Corner Playgroup, Armagh

My First Poem

My name is Chloe and I go to preschool,
My best friend is Samuel, who is really cool.
I watch Cinderella on TV,
Playing and colouring in is lots of fun for me.
I just love ham to eat,
And sometimes Nanny's tart for a treat.
Pink is a colour I like a lot,
My hairdresser is the best present I ever got.
My favourite person is Daddy, who is a gem,
So this, my first poem, is just for them!

Chloe Deering (4)
Tiny Tots Corner Playgroup, Armagh

My First Poem

My name is Dylan and I go to preschool,
My best friend is Anna, who is really cool.
I watch Golden Bear on TV,
Playing on my tablet that Santa brought is lots of fun for me.
I just love chicken and chips from KFC to eat,
And sometimes sweets for a treat.
Purple is a colour I like a lot,
My microphone is the best present I ever got.
My favourite person is Josh, who is a gem,
So this, my first poem, is just for them!

Dylan Robinson (4)

Tiny Tots Corner Playgroup, Armagh

My First Poem

My name is **Samuel** and I go to preschool,
My best friend is **Anna**, who is really cool.
I watch **tractors** on TV,
Playing **with New Hollands** is lots of fun for me.
I just love **carrots** to eat,
And sometimes **chocolate** for a treat.
Blue is a colour I like a lot,
My **New Holland tractor** is the best present
I ever got.
My favourite person is **Granny Elizabeth**,
who is a gem,
So this, my first poem, is just for them!

Samuel Gillespie (4)
Tiny Tots Corner Playgroup, Armagh

My First Poem

My name is Jaida and I go to preschool,
My best friend is Miyah, who is really cool.
I watch Tiny Pop on TV,
Playing with Thomas is lots of fun for me.
I just love spaghetti to eat,
And sometimes sweeties for a treat.
Blue is a colour I like a lot,
My crinky cronky truck is the best present I ever got.
My favourite person is Mommy, who is a gem,
So this, my first poem, is just for them!

Jaida Allam (3)
Voyage @ Flash Ley, Stafford

My First Poem

My name is Conor and I go to preschool,
My best friend is Mommy, who is really cool.
I watch PAW Patrol on TV,
Playing with PAW Patrol toys is lots of fun for me.
I just love sausages to eat,
And sometimes sweets for a treat.
Red is a colour I like a lot,
My PAW Patrol toy is the best present I ever got.
My favourite person is Mommy, who is a gem,
So this, my first poem, is just for them!

Conor Richard Norman Robinson (3)
Voyage @ Flash Ley, Stafford

My First Poem

My name is **Abbie** and I go to preschool,
My best friend is **Anna**, who is really cool.
I watch **Peppa Pig** on TV,
Playing **with my Peppa toys** is lots of fun for me.
I just love **dinosaurs** to eat,
And sometimes **chocolate** for a treat.
Blue is a colour I like a lot,
My **Bumblebee** is the best present I ever got.
My favourite person is **Daddy**, who is a gem,
So this, my first poem, is just for them!

Abbie Grace Judith Davis (3)
Voyage @ Flash Ley, Stafford

My First Poem

My name is **Maisy** and I go to preschool,
My best friend is **Mommy**, who is really cool.
I watch **Elsa** on TV,
Playing **with dollies** is lots of fun for me.
I just love **crumpets** to eat,
And sometimes **ice cream** for a treat.
Pink is a colour I like a lot,
My **Elsa doll** is the best present I ever got.
My favourite person is **Mommy**, who is a gem,
So this, my first poem, is just for them!

Maisy Michelle McCracken (3)
Voyage @ Flash Ley, Stafford

My First Poem

My name is **Saffron** and I go to preschool,
My best friend is **Grace**, who is really cool.
I watch **Chipmunks** on TV,
Playing **and clapping** is lots of fun for me.
I just love **Cheestrings** to eat,
And sometimes **Barny Bears** for a treat.
Black is a colour I like a lot,
My **iPuppies** are the best present I ever got.
My favourite people are **Daddy and Mummy**, who are gems,
So this, my first poem, is just for them!

Saffron Sheila Brenda Lowe (4)

Voyage @ Flash Ley, Stafford

My First Poem

My name is Grace and I go to preschool,
My best friend is Erin, who is really cool.
I watch Masha and the Bear on TV,
Playing the shopping game is lots of fun for me.
I just love peas and carrots to eat,
And sometimes sweeties for a treat.
Purple is a colour I like a lot,
My car game is the best present I ever got.
My favourite person is Mommy, who is a gem,
So this, my first poem, is just for them!

Grace Ghaley (3)
Voyage @ Flash Ley, Stafford

My First Poem

My name is **Niamh** and I go to Voyage,
My best friend is **Maymi** who is really funny.
I watch **Princess Sophia** on TV,
Playing **with toys** is lots of fun for me.
I just love **pasta** to eat,
And sometimes **Chocolate** for a treat.
Pink is a colour I like a lot,
My **doll** is the best present I ever got.
My favourite person is **Eloisa**, who is a gem,
So this, my first poem, is just for them!

Niamh Capewell (3)

Voyage @ Flash Ley, Stafford

My First Poem

We hope you have enjoyed reading this book - and that you will continue to enjoy it in the coming years.

If you're a young writer who enjoys reading and creative writing, or the parent of an enthusiastic poet or story writer, do visit our websites, www.myfirstpoem.com and www.youngwriters.co.uk. Here you will find free competitions, workshops and games, as well as recommended reads, a poetry glossary and our blog.

If you would like to order further copies of this book, or any of our other titles, then please give us a call or visit www.myfirstpoem.com.

My First Poem
Remus House
Coltsfoot Drive
Peterborough
PE2 9BF

Tel: 01733 898110
info@myfirstpoem.com